Great Walks of Acadia National Park & Mount Desert Island

Revised Edition

Text by Robert Gillmore
Photographs by Eileen Oktavec

To Margaret O'Reilly Oktavec and Albert William Oktavec III, who made it all possible.

Great Walks ®

No. 1 in a series of full-color, pocket-size guides to the best walks in the world published by Great Walks Inc. Other Great Walks guides: *Great Walks of Southern Arizona, Great Walks of Big Bend National Park, Great Walks of the Great Smokies, Great Walks of Yosemite National Park, Great Walks of Sequoia & Kings Canyon National Parks,* and *Great Walks of the Olympic Peninsula.* For more information on all Great Walks guides send $1 (refundable with your first order) to: Great Walks, PO Box 410, Goffstown, NH 03045.

Surf breaks over the smooth stones on the beach at ... Cove along the **Ocean Trail** *(Walk No. 3). ... the highest ocean cliffs on Mount Desert Island, ...ance.*

CONTENTS

Acknowledgments

We are grateful for the assistance of Deborah Wade of the National Park Service, Mike Raynor of the Acadia Corp. and Keith Miller of the Eastern National Park and Monument Association.

What Are Great Walks?

Great Walks invariably offer beautiful and interesting world-class scenery and excellent views in the most picturesque places on earth.

Great Walks are also shorter and easier than the typical hike or climb. They're usually less than five miles long. They can be walked in a day or less. And they're usually on smooth, firm, dry and, most important, *gently graded* trails. (Long, arduous, sweaty treks up rough, steep, rocky trails are *not* Great Walks!)

What Are
Great Walks Guides?

Great Walks guides carefully describe and, with beautiful full-color photographs, lavishly illustrate the world's Great Walks.

Unlike many walking guides, which describe *every* trail in a region, Great Walks describe only the *best* walks, the happy few that will especially delight you with their beauty.

Unlike many guides, which give you mainly directions, Great Walks guides carefully describe *all* the major features of every Great Walk so you can know, in advance, *precisely* what the Walk has to offer and exactly *why* it's worth your time to take it.

After all, your leisure time is valuable. In your lifetime you can walk on only a fraction of the hundreds of thousands of miles of trails in the world. Why not walk only the best?

For your convenience Great Walks guides are an easy-to-use and easy-to-carry pocket size and their covers are film laminated for extra protection against wear and tear.

Foreword:
New England's
Natural Theme Park
— and How to Enjoy It

A fortuitous combination of natural and man-made circumstances makes the walking in and around Acadia National Park among the best in the world.

The most important circumstance is that Acadia National Park is a kind of natural theme park in which the most beautiful elements of New England's landscape — ledge-topped mountains, pristine forested lakes and rockbound, island-dotted seacoast — are all gathered together, seemingly for the convenience of vacationers. In Acadia, the perennial question "Shall we go to the mountains, the lakes or the ocean?" does not apply. In Acadia you have it all.

Much of Acadia's magnificent scenery can be seen on long, glorious views from the park's mountain trails. These views are a happy result of three things: Acadia has some of the highest summits on the entire east coast of the Americas; most of the park's tallest peaks have bare, rocky summits; and most of the trees near those summits are short.

But even though Acadia's mountains are high enough and bare enough for often-nonstop views, they're low enough to be easily climbed. Cadillac Mountain, for example, is the highest peak on the North Atlantic Coast, but it's only 1,530 feet high.

What's more, most of Acadia's mountains are long ridges, so they can be ascended on gentle grades.

Although Acadia National Park is small, there are 29 Great Walks, plus three Honorable Mentions, in or around it. Almost no place else in the world offers so many Great Walks in so small an area. Moreover, all the Walks on Mount Desert Island (where most of the park is located) are just a short drive apart and few are more than 15 minutes from your hotel or campground. Almost nowhere else can you get to so many Great Walks so quickly and so easily.

Because all the Walks are in or near the national park, many of the roads you'll be driving on are well sited and landscaped and most of the scenery is otherwise unspoiled. On the Park Loop Road, for example, you'll be struck not only by its many ocean views but also by the fact that there are no telephone poles or fence posts. Wires are underground and handsome granite rocks do the work of guardrails. The only manmade thing in your view is the pavement.

Finally, Mount Desert Island's creature comforts are many and handy. Bar Harbor teems with motels, hotels, guest houses and bed-and-breakfasts—old and new, plain and very fancy. Bar Harbor also has many good restaurants and it's close to many of the island's Walks. In Acadia, a fine lunch or dinner is never more than a short drive away. In fact, the area is home to so many good things that you'd want to come here even if you never set one foot on one trail.

The Walks described below will show you the area's most beautiful scenery.

All but four Great Walks as well as all three

Honorable Mentions are on Mount Desert Island. Walks No. 1-3 take you along dramatic seacoast on level paths. Walk No. 4 goes across Sand Beach and the windswept coastal overlook known as Great Head. Walks No. 5-7 and 31 take you along the shores of lovely mountain-rimmed lakes and ponds. Walks No 8-10 are short excursions through four outstanding works of landscaping. Walks No. 11-25, 29 and 32 take you to the tops of 20 different mountains or other promontories for some of the best mountain, lake and ocean views you'll ever see.

Four of the Great Walks—Nos. 26-29—are on Isle au Haut, a hilly, spruce-covered island about 14 miles off Mount Desert Island. (Samuel de Champlain named it the *haut*, or high, island because, unlike the other, low islands in the area, Isle au Haut has a central ridge that's more than 500 feet above sea level at its highest point.) Walks No. 26-28 follow the six-mile-long island's wild southern and western coasts. Walk No. 29 takes you up Duck Harbor Mountain for a series of broad ocean views.

Unlike Mount Desert Island, which is connected to the mainland by a short bridge, Isle au Haut is accessible only by boat. From the second Monday in June to the second Saturday in September, the Isle au Haut Co. ferries passengers from Stonington, on the coast, to Duck Harbor Landing, on Isle au Haut. Duck Harbor Landing is about .2 miles from Western Head Road, where all four of the island's Great Walks begin. However, the ferry doesn't reach the landing until 11 A.M. and its last run back to Stonington leaves at 6 P.M., which gives you only seven hours on the island—not enough to do all four Walks.

If you want to spend more time on the island, you have four choices: You can keep taking the two-hour, $24-round-trip ferry ride to Duck Harbor Landing. You can camp in one of five wooden lean-tos near the landing. You can look for a house on the island to rent. Or you can stay at the island's only inn: the Keeper's House.

The inn is a rare delight. It's the handsome former residence of the "keeper" of the adjacent lighthouse. The lighthouse has been automated by the Coast Guard and the residence and its outbuildings are now a cozy six-bedroom inn heated with wood stoves and lit by candles and kerosene lamps. Yes, there's no electricity. But there *are* hot showers, and the inn's home-cooked breakfasts, dinners and box lunches are creative, its decor (large windows and light-filled, pastel-painted rooms with white-painted antiques) is pleasant, and the ambience is mellow. The Keeper's House also rents bicycles on which you can ride to the trailheads. For more information call 207-367-2261. For more information about the ferry call 207-367-5193. For camping information call the park headquarters at 207-288-3338.

None of these Walks is strenuous. In fact, ten of them—Nos. 1, 2, 5, 6, 8-10, 19, 25 and 31—are either easy or very easy and 11 others—Nos. 3, 4, 7, 11, 13, 17, 20, 22, 24, 27 and 30—while not exactly easy, are nevertheless undemanding. The 11 remaining Walks—Nos. 12, 14-16, 18, 21, 23, 26, 28, 29 and 32—are moderate.

Most of the Walks are on smooth or fairly smooth trails and on either level or gently graded paths. The few, brief exceptions to this rule—on Walks No. 7,

14-16, 23 and 29—are noted. The typical Walk is only about one to three miles long. (The *longest* Walk—No. 26—is only 6.6 miles long.)

How long does each Walk take? That depends, of course, on how fast you walk. But a very rough rule of thumb is: one hour per mile. If you walk faster and don't pause to enjoy the views (see below), the time per mile is less. The average Walk takes just a few hours, the longest one no more than seven or eight hours. Depending on your speed, it takes about 10 to 14 days to do all of them.

In general, the very best Walks are those that take you up mountains and along the ocean. Of these, the crème de la crème are Nos. 1, 3, 4, 11, 12, 14, 18, 19 and 24-27. Two other Walks, Nos. 9 and 10, take you to splendid gardens.

What's the best time to take these Walks? In late spring and fall the weather is usually cool—just right for walking—the park is uncrowded and hotels charge off-season rates. Fall, however, has an added bonus: the leaves are turning color and the blueberry bushes on the ledges are solid drifts of deep red. But because most park visitors seldom stray far from their cars, trails are rarely crowded at any time, even in the busy summer season. (And the blueberries, by the way, are ripe in August.)

Here are some tips to help you get the most out of these Walks:

▶This guide tells you *exactly* what each Walk has to offer. Take advantage of it by reading it before you take *any* Walks. That way you'll be best able to select Walks that most closely suit your taste.

▶Carry the guide on all Walks. (It'll fit easily in

any pocket.) It tells you how to reach the trailhead and gives you precise directions for each Walk, as well as detailed descriptions of what you'll see.

▶ The Walks start where they start, stop where they stop and go where they go for two reasons: (1) the routes we describe provide the best walking in the area; (2) any other routes are more difficult, less scenic or both. The park has more than 100 miles of hiking trails and 50 miles of carriage roads but only the routes described below are Great Walks or Honorable Mentions.

▶ Most of the park's trailhead parking areas are marked by distinctive brown signs with white letters. The beginnings of trails are signed with wooden posts with incised letters; junctions are marked by horizontal wood signs attached to wooden posts; all trail signs indicate distances (of occasionally disputable accuracy). Summits are marked by wooden signs indicating both the name of the mountain or peak and its elevation. Trails are blazed by (usually) blue paint on rocks or trees and by cairns (small rock piles) on ledges. Most trails are easy to follow and in any event we tell you everything you need to know to find your way. A map, therefore, is not necessary for *directions*. But a detailed, easy-to-read topographical map is very helpful in identifying mountains, islands, bays and other landmarks. The best topographic map of Mount Desert Island — the one that indicates the largest number of features in the clearest way — is published by DeLorme and sold for about $8 at the park Visitor Center and other outlets. The best map of Isle au Haut is published by the Park Service and is available free on the ferry to the island. Also helpful for getting around the area is the park's *Official Map and Guide*. Like all similar National Park Service publications, it clearly and attractively indicates all roads in and near the park, as well as trails and other natural and manmade features. It's yours for free at the Visitor Center and the entrance station on the Park Loop Road.

►Unless you're in excellent condition (and few people are) do your body a favor: Whenever possible, do the Walks in order of difficulty, easiest ones first. That way each Walk will help prepare you to take the harder one that follows. Ideally, you'll be able to progress from short, easy Walks to longer, harder ones with little difficulty.

►Any comfortable walking shoes are fine for Walks that follow smooth paths (Nos. 1-3, 5, 8-10, 19 and 31). For other walks we recommend the greater support and protection of above-the-ankle hiking boots. To avoid unnecessary discomfort (including blisters) make sure your footwear fits and is broken in before you start walking.

►Long-range views are clearest on sunny days, so do the mountain Walks in fair weather. Save the garden Walks (Nos. 9 and 10) and those with short-range views (Nos. 6, 7 and 31) for cloudy days.

►We suggest you carry rain gear and wear waterproof hiking boots whenever wet weather is imminent. For best protection, we recommend a lightweight waterproof hooded jacket and pants. The most comfortable rain garments are made of "breathable" Goretex fabric, which keeps rain out but also lets perspiration escape.

►Carry water on longer Walks. It will taste best if

you carry it in ceramic canteens, such as the French-made Tournus, rather than plastic or metal bottles. If you have access to a refrigerator, here's a way to keep the water cold: The night before a Walk pour just an inch or so of water in the canteen and lay it on its side in the freezer, leaving the top open to make sure the canteen doesn't crack when the water freezes and expands. Next morning fill the canteen with cold water. The ice already inside will keep the water cold.

►Never drink water from any stream or spring without filtering it or treating it with purifying tablets. The risk of an attack of *giardia lamblia* is too great to drink untreated water.

►Never urinate or defecate within 100 feet of brooks or lakes and don't wash yourself in them. (Even biodegradable soap pollutes lakes and stream if used directly in them.)

►It's obvious but it bears repeating: Binoculars enable you to see what you can't see, or see as well, without them (bald eagles, for example). A high-powered, lightweight pair is worth carrying.

►Use enough sunscreen to keep the exposed parts of your body from burning and wear something to keep the sun out of your eyes. We favor a wide-brimmed hat or a sun visor over tinted sunglasses, which substitute a tinted view of the world for the real one. A hat or visor also helps keep you cool by protecting much of your face from the sun.

►Mosquitoes and other flying insects can sometimes be a pesty problem in warmer weather. Carry some repellent, just in case.

►Be sure to begin each Walk early enough so you can finish it comfortably before dark.

►On longer Walks, carry a small flashlight in case you can't get back before dark, as well as some toilet paper and Band-Aids.

►Walks No. 5-7, 13, 15, 16, 18 and 30 are wholly or partly on carriage roads, which are popular bike routes. Most bikers will give you ample warning when they pass but some simply whizz by at astounding speeds. So it's a good idea to look out for bikes on carriage roads, especially when you're "changing lanes" (i.e., moving to the left or right).

►Remember that the world's only constant is change. The locations of the lakes and mountains on these walks won't vary from year to year but anything subject to human control — trail routes, parking lots, signs and so on — can change. Be alert for trail reroutings and follow signs.

►Above all, remember that a Great Walk is mainly an aesthetic activity, not an athletic one. Its primary purpose is not to give you exercise (although exercise you will surely get) but to expose you to exceptional natural beauty. Walk slowly enough to savor it. Most people walk too fast. Don't make their mistake. You no more want to rush through these Walks than you want to rush through the Louvre.

Great Walks of
Mount Desert Island

1 The Shore Path

This .5-mile round trip is a leisurely promenade on a wide, smooth, gravelly path along the top of seawalls at the very edge of Frenchman Bay in Bar Harbor. On its shore side the Walk offers intimate looks at the inns and summer homes for which Bar Harbor is famous. On its ocean side the Walk provides uninterrupted vistas of the blue waters of the bay, dotted by the unspoiled rockbound, spruce-topped Porcupine Islands.

The Shore Path begins at the town pier at the end of Main Street. The path isn't marked but it's easy to find. Face the handsome, gray-shingled Bar Harbor Inn, just east of the pier. To your left is a stony beach. To your right is the lawn of tiny Agamont Park. Between the beach and the park is an asphalt sidewalk heading toward the ocean side of the inn. The sidewalk is the beginning of the Walk.

The path curves along the beach, past a long wooden pier at which excursion boats dock. Red geraniums grow in boxes on the pier railings. The island off to your left and closest to shore is Bar Island. To the right of Bar Island is Sheep Porcupine Island.

The pier is the first and last thing on the Shore Path that stands between you and the ocean. From here until the end of the Walk, the only things to the left of the path will be rocky shores and blue ocean. On your right you'll pass the rolling lawn of the Bar Harbor Inn and then the yellow-and-white umbrellas shading the tables of Gatsby's Terrace, the inn's outdoor dining area. The inn's large, bow-fronted dining room is above the terrace.

The path changes from asphalt to gravel and quickly bends around a small point. Now you'll be able to see all four Porcupine Islands: from left to right, Sheep Porcupine; Burnt Porcupine, farther offshore; Long Porcupine, even farther offshore — its long side is perpendicular to you, so it'll look larger but not much longer than the others — and Bald Porcupine, nearer to shore, at the eastern end of a long, low rock breakwater. The islands were named Porcupine not because porcupines lived on them but because — with their low, slightly humpy shapes, their covering of pointy quill-like spruce trees, and the granite rock at the ends of the islands that resembles noses — they *look* like porcupines. Or at least to some people they do.

Still more islands, and Schoodic Peninsula behind them, are visible on the other side of Frenchman Bay. Almost straight ahead of you, over the breakwater, you can make out the white-and-orange lighthouse on Egg Rock, nearly two miles away.

After leaving the last gray-shingled building of the Bar Harbor Inn, the path passes Grant Park (also known as Albert Meadow), a tiny, grassy public park outfitted with benches and picnic tables and shaded by a huge birch tree. A sign at the southern edge of the park explains that the Shore Path was created more than 100 years ago "by the original owners of the private properties on which it is located" and that the present owners "are pleased to continue this tradition."

Next you'll see Balance Rock Inn on your right. A sign beside the trail explains that the inn was built in 1903 as a summer residence "for Scottish railroad magnate Alexander Maitland and his family and servants." The pleasing neoclassical revival building overlooks a wide lawn and its namesake, Balance Rock, a 6-foot-wide, 15-foot-high boulder that seems to rest precariously on the stony beach. Like Bubble Rock (Walk No. 17), its uncertain position is an illusion: No one has come close to pushing it over.

After passing an apple tree on your left and patches of Queen Anne's lace on your right, the Walk runs along the left of a picturesque weathered board fence. To the right of the fence are the back yards of private homes.

The path then passes a Tudor revival mansion. A discreet sign on a white arbor identifies the imposing structure as the Breakwater. Like the Balance Rock Inn, which was built one year earlier, the Breakwater was originally a summer "cottage" for a wealthy family. Now it's a sumptuously appointed bed-and-breakfast.

After crossing a short wooden bridge, the Shore Path ends abruptly at a chain-link fence. Turn

---

*White sailboats and rocky, spruce-tipped islands in the blue waters of Frenchman Bay, seen from the **Shore Path** (Walk No. 1) in Bar Harbor. Bar Island is on the left.* ▶

around here and enjoy the views again as you retrace your steps to the beginning of the Walk.

If, perchance, you want to get to Main Street from the Shore Path, you can do so from three places. At the end of the path you can take a right and follow the short unpaved road to Wayman Lane, which leads to Main Street. Or you can leave the path at the southern end of the weathered board fence (not far from the Breakwater) and follow a short path to Hancock Street, which also leads to Main Street. Or you can cross Albert Meadow and follow a short street to Main Street.

Travel Tip: You can make the Walk's views last even longer if you stop for lunch or a drink at Gatsby's Terrace, which we think has the best sea view of any restaurant on the island. From your table you can gaze at the flotilla of white boats in the harbor and the islands beyond them.

2 Dorr Point & Compass Harbor

This easy one-mile Walk takes you to the end of a long, narrow point with a sweeping ocean view that ranges from secluded Compass Harbor to Odgen Point to the Porcupine Islands to Schoodic Peninsula to the Egg Rock lighthouse. You'll also explore some quiet pebble beaches and the intriguing remains of the estate of George B. Dorr, a founder of Acadia National Park and its first superintendent.

This Walk begins at an unmarked parking area on Route 3, exactly one mile south of the intersection of Main and Mount Desert streets in downtown Bar Harbor. As you drive out of Bar Harbor, the ledgy face of Champlain Mountain (Walk No. 12) rises directly ahead of you. You'll pass the stone walls, gates and gatehouses of present and former ocean-front mansions on your left. About .5 miles after passing Cromwell Harbor Road on your right, you'll reach the small gravel trailhead parking area, on your left. (If you pass the Ocean Drive Motor Court, also on the left, you've gone a couple of hundred feet too far.)

The trail is an old road. A brown-and-white park service sign on the gate says "Fire Road/Do Not Block." Large granite rocks stand on either side of the gate and a nine-foot-tall rhododendron, the vestige of old landscaping, grows on the right.

The level road passes through an open, sunny grove of large maples, oaks and other hardwoods. You're now walking on the grounds of what was George Dorr's estate; try to imagine what these woods were like when he lived here.

In about 100 feet you'll cross a small brook; note the ruined walls along the stream on your left.

About 300 feet from the parking area the road forks. Go left and follow a slightly narrower road as it gently curves to the right, around low ledges on the right of the path. You'll soon start glimpsing the ocean through the trees.

About .2 miles from the parking lot you'll pass paths going to the left and right. Keep going straight ahead. You'll then see the round, 1,000-foot-wide Compass Harbor on your left.

The road narrows to a trail as it curves around the southern edge of the harbor and passes through a grassy clearing with an enormous, multi-trunked white pine on the right.

Then the path runs along the top of the narrow peninsula known as Dorr Point. In one place the steep slopes of the 50-foot-long point have been so eroded that the top of the peninsula is only six feet wide.

The path ends at jagged ledges at the end of the point. Now you're in the very center of a horseshoe-shaped band of water that stretches from Compass Harbor on your far left to the mouth of Frenchman Bay on your far right. Your vista, seen from left to right, begins at your left rear: that is, along Dorr Point, which is the southern arm of the shallow, usually placid harbor; then it runs along the concave rocky shore of the harbor to Ogden Point, which is the harbor's northern arm. Grassy, parklike Ogden Point is dotted with clumps of spruces and hardwood trees. Behind the point you can see the high eastern end of Bar Island. To the right of Bar Island and behind the *end* of Ogden Point is Sheep Porcupine Island; note the high granite "nose" on its eastern

The pebbly beach of **Compass Harbor** *(Walk No. 2). Spruce-topped Ogden Point is on the horizon on the left. Bald Porcupine Island is on the right.* ▶

end. To the right of Sheep Porcupine, and much farther away, is Burnt Porcupine Island. To the right of Burnt Porcupine, and less than a mile away, is Bald Porcupine Island, its steep, bare rock sides echoed by the tall pointed spruces above them. A long, rocky breakwater extends from Bald Porcupine Island almost all the way to the mouth of Cromwell Cove, which is just on the other side of Ogden Point. The tiny island of Rumkey is between Burnt and Bald Porcupine islands; Long Porcupine Island is hidden behind Bald Porcupine. Six miles away, across Frenchman Bay, is Schoodic Peninsula (note the water tower). To the right of the peninsula, at the mouth of Frenchman Bay, is Egg Rock lighthouse. Far to your right and just a couple of hundred feet away is a tiny pebble beach.

When you're ready, retrace your steps to the clearing with the big white pine. From there you can make three side trips: to the pebble beach farther south, to the head of Compass Harbor and to the ruins of Dorr's mansion.

If you want to go to the beach, simply walk through the trees along the shore; you'll reach the beach in a minute.

To get to the head of the harbor, start walking back to the parking area. Less than 100 feet from the clearing you'll come to the trails you passed on your way in. Follow the path on the right through the woods at the edge of the harbor. Between the trees on your right you'll see the harbor's gray ledges and rocky beaches. On the horizon you'll see Ogden Point and Burnt and Bald Porcupine islands.

The path ends at a granite bench beside a small

grassy clearing. You're now on the grounds of Nannau, a handsome, weathered brown-shingled mansion built as a summer "cottage" for a wealthy family in 1904. The mansion, a couple of hundred feet from the shore, is now a bed-and-breakfast inn.

Because the inn is private, turn around here and retrace your steps to the clearing.

To reach the ruins of the Dorr estate, follow the faint path to the right of the big pine. You'll walk barely 150 feet before the trail curves to the right.

Suddenly, in the middle of the woods, you'll see a long flight of granite steps dead ahead. Follow the 42 steps up the slope to a brick-and-stone ruin. At the top of the steps are the remains of a terrace, its brick floor laid in a handsome herringbone pattern. When the trees were smaller you could see Frenchman Bay from here. Note the large rhododendrons—more remains of the original landscaping—on the south side of the ruin.

When you're ready to continue, find the path on the southwest side of the former terrace and follow it through the woods. In a few hundred feet the trail splits. Take the righthand fork and follow the path as it curves to the right.

You'll quickly come to the junction, about 300 feet from the parking area, that you passed on your way to Compass Harbor. Take a left and retrace your steps to your car.

3 The Ocean Trail

This undemanding four-mile round trip follows perhaps the most interesting two miles of seashore in Acadia National Park. Its almost uninterrupted views include Sand Beach, Great Head, Schoodic Peninsula, Western Point, Newport and Otter coves, the 30-foot-high sea stack in Monument Cove, the Beehive and Gorham, Dorr, Champlain and Cadillac mountains. You'll walk along the top of Otter Cliffs—the highest ocean-edge cliffs in the park—and pass the well-named Thunder Hole, where the surf booms as it crashes into a narrow tunnel in the coast ledge.

To get to the trailhead, take the Park Loop Road to Sand Beach, which is about nine miles south of the park Visitor Center in Hulls Cove (where the Loop Road starts) and about three miles south of the intersection of the Loop Road and Route 3 south of Bar Harbor. The path begins at the southern end of the parking lot closest to the Loop Road.

The first half of the Ocean Trail follows the shore side of the Loop Road. If you're in a hurry you can drive along this part of the shore and pick up the path

Otter Cliffs at sunrise, seen from the **Ocean Trail** *(Walk No. 3).* ▶

farther down the road. However, the sights, sounds and smells of the park are better on foot. One day we saw a deer in the spruce-and-pine woods on the other side of the road; no one in the passing cars seemed to notice it.

The path here is smooth gravel, mostly level and often just a few feet from the ocean. Short, well-worn side paths take you over the rough-chiseled ledges that are even closer to the sea. Low pitch pines and bayberry bushes grow between the ledges and, in the fall, dozens of eider ducks float on the swells below.

To your left you have long views of Sand Beach and the rockbound, evergreen-covered Great Head (Walk No. 4) on the other side of Newport Cove. Off the mouth of the cove is the low, wave-washed rock islet known (appropriately) as Old Soaker. To your right is 525-foot Gorham Mountain (Walk No. 11).

About .5 miles from Sand Beach you'll come to Thunder Hole. As a sign at the site explains, the thunderlike "boom" you hear is caused when waves rush into a long, narrow tunnel in the rock, sealing off and compressing the air inside. Thunder Hole makes the most noise on an incoming tide, about three hours after low tide. Check local newspapers for the tide schedule. Cement steps take you not only to the top of Thunder Hole but also to a waterside, observation platform from which you can see Sand Beach on your left, Otter Cliffs on your right and Schoodic Peninsula straight ahead.

In another 1,000 feet or so the trail passes tiny Monument Cove. Follow the very short side path to the overlook on the left of the trail. The beach below is composed of thousands of the smoothest rocks you'll ever see. Many look like huge eggs or giant peas. Also on the beach is a remarkable 30-foot-high column of rock, known as a sea stack, after which the cove is named. Sea stacks are carved by the surf from much larger pieces of rock and eventually they'll be worn away too.

Be alert for patches of poison ivy beside the trail as you approach another cove. When you reach this little bay, follow another very short side path to an overlook where you'll have a close view of Otter Cliffs.

About a mile from the trailhead the Loop Road moves slightly away from both the path and the shore and the trail heads into a cool, lush, shady spruce-and-fir grove. Ahead of you, on your left, Otter Cliffs loom 100 feet above the water. As you approach the cliffs, you can hear the crackle of waves breaking over stony beaches beneath you. As you get closer to the crest of the cliffs, very short side trails let you get close to the edge. (Approach carefully; there's no railing.) Peer cautiously over the edge of the cliffs (lying on your stomach) and you'll see stone beaches and white surf below. From this spot you can also see, to your far left, the ridges of Cadillac and Dorr mountains (Walk No. 19), the south ridge of Champlain Mountain (Walk No. 12), Gorham Mountain and the bare rock of the 520-foot Beehive. You can also look back to Sand Beach and Old Soaker and across to Great Head.

Now the path quickly reaches a small asphalt observation platform at the foot of a short flight of granite steps. After ascending the steps the trail passes between two low, concentric granite walls.

You're now about 120 feet above sea level, the highest point of the Walk. You can sometimes see ducks and cormorants diving in the ocean far below you and you'll hear the pleasant clang of a bell on a green buoy offshore. Turn around and you'll see Gorham and Champlain mountains and the Beehive.

The trail then switches back and forth down stone steps, closer to the ocean. Soon you'll pass, on your right, a bronze plaque that says: "These groves of spruce and fir, these granite ledges, the magnificent window on the sea, were given to the United States by John D. Rockefeller, Jr." (Actually you'll probably notice the plaque only on your return trip because it's easy to miss when you're walking the trail from north to south.)

The path quickly reaches Otter Point, a pleasant, grassy, spruce-shaded headland, just a few feet above the ocean, that seems to be made for picnicking, dawdling and nature watching. About 4.5 miles to the south is the half-mile-wide, 92-foot-high Baker Island. To the right of Baker are the flatter Cranberry Isles.

A vertical wooden post sign marks a short dirt road that connects the Ocean Trail to the Loop Road. Keep left at this junction and follow the path around the point to the narrow, mile-long Otter Cove. Here your view includes not only Baker and the Cranberry Isles but also Western Point, on the

A dusting of early morning snow on the Otter Cliffs and on the smooth stones of a beach along the **Ocean Trail** *(Walk No. 3).* ▶

western shore of Otter Cove, and, on your right, the low triple-arched bridge on which the Loop Road crosses Otter Cove about .7 miles to the north. The Ocean Trail ends where stone steps go up to the Loop Road opposite the western entrance to the Otter Point parking area. From here you retrace your steps to your car. On your return trip, the light, the tide and especially your views will be different. You won't be seeing quite the same thing twice.

4 Sand Beach & Great Head

This undemanding Walk, barely a mile and a quarter long, offers stirring ocean and mountain views. You'll see the Beehive, Otter and Cadillac cliffs and Gorham Mountain across Newport Cove, Schoodic Peninsula across Frenchman Bay, the Egg Rock lighthouse, and Baker Island and Little Cranberry Island five miles offshore.

Sand Beach is often separated from Great Head peninsula by a tiny channel that links Newport Cove to the lagoon behind the beach. At high tide, this channel is usually too deep to cross without getting your feet wet. For the driest crossing, take this Walk when the tide is lowest. (Local newspapers publish tide tables.)

Like Walk No. 3, this outing begins at Sand Beach, which is on the Park Loop Road, about nine miles south of the park Visitor Center and about three miles south of the intersection of the Loop Road and Route 3, just south of Bar Harbor.

Park in the lower lot, the one closest to the ocean. Look back toward the Loop Road and you'll see the pink granite cliff of the Beehive rising above a forest of white birches. The steep eastern slope of Champlain Mountain (Walk No. 12) is to the right.

Walk to the southern end of the parking lot—the end closest to the sea—and start descending the granite steps to Sand Beach. A plaque near the top of the steps explains how the park's only sand beach was formed—it's a mixture of finely ground rock and a "high percentage of shell fragments and other remains of marine animals." The beach is popular for strolling, sunning, picnicking and sea watching but not for swimming: the water is *cold,* even in the summer.

The granite steps take you down to the western end of the 1,000-foot-long beach. From here you walk toward the Great Head peninsula, at the eastern end of the beach. You'll pass sand dunes and a rustic rail fence on your left. On your right is Newport Cove. On your far right are the Otter Cliffs on Otter Point (Walk No. 3). Just to the left of the point is Baker Island. At the mouth of the cove is the tiny rock island known as Old Soaker. Look behind you occasionally as you walk across the beach and you'll see, from left to right, Gorham Mountain (Walk No. 11) and Cadillac Cliffs on its lower slope; the Beehive and the near vertical east wall of Champlain Mountain.

Soon you'll come to the channel separating the beach and the dunes from the Great Head peninsula. On your left you'll see up the narrow, sinuous, 1,000-foot-long lagoon, surrounded by marshes. On the other side of the channel is the post marking the Great Head Trail.

Cross the channel at its shallowest point. (If you can't cross without soaking your shoes and socks, take them off and cross barefoot. You don't want to walk in wet footwear.) Now walk up the granite steps behind the trail post and you'll come to a small grassy clearing. On your left you'll see a six-foot-wide mill-stone flat on the ground. On your right you'll see the beginnings of three trails.

The Great Head Trail is on the far right. It switches back and forth up the ledgy slope, through spruces and dwarf white birches. There's more ledge than bare earth here, so follow the discreet blue blazes to keep on the path.

After a few hundred feet the Great Head Trail splits. Follow the right fork (you'll return on the left one) and you'll quickly reach the top of the Great Head ridge. Here you'll have exhilarating views of the ocean on both sides of the trail. To your left (east) is Frenchman Bay and Schoodic Peninsula. On your right is a bird's-eye view of Sand Beach, the lagoon and Newport Cove. Opposite the cove are Gorham Mountain and the tall, ledgy hump of the Beehive.

Sand Beach, the lagoon and the steep, 520-foot hump known as the Beehive seen from **Great Head** *(Walk No. 4).*
◄

Frenchman Bay drops from sight as the trail leads to the southern edge of the peninsula, but there are uninterrupted views of Newport Cove, Gorham Mountain and Otter Point. The essence of the relentless beauty of this coast is its almost gross simplicity. This part of Mount Desert Island is neither delicate nor subtle. It's a rough, wild place where steep, bare granite rock and dark evergreen forests rise steeply out of a frothy sea.

As you reach the southern edge of Great Head, the surf gets rougher and higher. Waves turn to foam as they crash into the immense, jagged rock headlands and the pure white froth contrasts powerfully with the gray ledges. In the fall, flocks of eider ducks drift up and down on the swells.

Soon the trail reaches the highest point on Great Head, a 145-foot pinnacle near its southeastern shore. Here, on the stone ruins of a teahouse built by the wealthy Satterlee family, you can see the ocean in three directions. To the east, five miles across Frenchman Bay, is Schoodic Peninsula. In the mouth of the bay is Egg Rock lighthouse. To the north, on the edge of the bay, is Oak Hill Cliff; north of the cliff is Schooner Head. Still farther north are the Porcupine Islands off Bar Harbor. To the west, over low spruces, you can see, from right to left: Champlain Mountain, the Beehive, Gorham Mountain and Otter Point. The top of the long ridge of Cadillac Mountain (Walks No. 19 and 20) is on the horizon. To the south is Baker Island and, to the right of Baker, the eastern end of Little Cranberry Island.

From the teahouse ruins the path heads north,

away from the ocean and through scrub spruces and an elegant beech grove. In about 300 yards, when you just begin to glimpse the ocean again on your right, the trail splits. Take a left.

In another 300 yards or so the trail quickly climbs to the wide, flat top of the magnificent Great Head ridge. As you ascend the ridge, look behind you; you'll start to get wide views of Frenchman Bay. On the ridge itself you'll have exhilarating views of *both* sides of the peninsula. Stroll slowly through the scrub pines on this wonderful viewpoint. Make the experience last. If you have time, have a picnic.

As you start descending the west side of the peninsula, the path will rejoin the trail on which you climbed up the ridge. From here, retrace your steps to the parking area and enjoy the views of—and from—Sand Beach again.

5 Eagle Lake

This very easy 1.3-mile round trip presents a series of dramatic lake-and-mountain vistas from a smooth, nearly level carriage road. Across Eagle Lake—Mount Desert Island's second-largest body of fresh water after Long Pond (Walk No. 31)—you'll have continuing views of some of the island's highest peaks—Cadillac, Pemetic, Penobscot and Sargent mountains—as well as Conners Nubble and the North and South Bubbles.

Carriage roads are popular bike routes and some cyclists will pass you at amazing speeds. Most will give you warning but it's still a good idea to look behind you before "changing lanes" (i. e., moving to the left or right).

The Walk begins at a parking area on the north side of Route 233, 2.3 miles west of the intersection of Routes 3 and 233 in Bar Harbor.

From the parking area you'll see, on the other side of Route 233, a tiny inlet in the northwestern end of Eagle Lake. On the horizon, across the two-mile-long lake, is a dramatic mountainscape. In the center is the haystack-shaped hump of 1,247-foot Pemetic Mountain (Walk No. 14), the park's fourth-highest peak. Left of Pemetic is the low valley of Bubble Pond (Walk No. 6) and rising steeply to the left of the valley is the western slope of 1,530-foot Cadillac Mountain (Walks No. 19 and 20), the park's highest summit. To the right of Pemetic is another low valley, Jordan Carry; to the right of the valley are the steep eastern slopes of the Bubbles (Walks No. 17 and 18).

From the west side of the parking area a short path takes you immediately to a carriage road, which crosses Route 233 under a large, handsome stone-arch bridge, one of 17 such structures on the carriage

The twin peaks of the **Bubbles** *(Walks No. 17 and 18) seen from the blueberry fields on the southern end of* **Jordan Pond** *(Walk No. 7).*
◄

roads. Follow the carriage road under Route 233. On the other side of the highway take a left onto another carriage road and you'll immediately come to the head of the inlet you saw from the parking area. Now you'll have a closer view of the peaks and valleys you saw earlier.

Walk past the inlet and the wooded point to the east of it and you'll quickly come to a boat-launch area. Here your view is even wider. You can see everything you saw before, plus the tops of the 766-foot South Bubble and the wider, higher 872-foot North Bubble; 1,194-foot Penobscot Mountain (Walk No. 15), the park's fifth-highest peak, behind the Bubbles; and the higher, longer ridge of 1,373-foot Sargent Mountain (Walk No. 16), the park's second-highest summit, on the right. If the light is right, you'll also see the ledgy knob of the 588-foot Conners Nubble (Walk No. 18), whose steep sides appear to rise almost straight out of the lake below Penobscot Mountain. You may also see Bubble Rock on the horizon, just left of the summit of the South Bubble, and you'll probably see cars going up the road to the top of Cadillac Mountain.

The road passes through trees and quickly comes to a third viewpoint. Then it runs through still more trees before coming to a fourth clearing, where you can see even more of Sargent Mountain, on the right.

After passing through more woods the road reaches yet another clearing. Here a side road goes to the right and in about 100 feet brings you to a small brick building beside a dam at the edge of Eagle Lake. The lake is Bar Harbor's water supply; the brick building is the Bar Harbor Water Company's pumping station. The wide stream that begins at the dam is Duck Brook; it flows into Frenchman Bay just north of Bar Harbor.

After you've enjoyed the view from this spot, go back to the carriage road and follow it again into the woods. You'll cross Duck Brook almost immediately and catch still more views of the mountains through the trees.

Then the road curves to the right, around the northeast corner of the lake, and you'll have another vista across the water. But now you can see only Sargent Mountain to the east, the low, rounded 724-foot McFarland Mountain, northwest of the lake, and the brick pumping station on your right.

Turn around here and head back toward your car. When you reach the boat-launch area, you can keep following the road back to your car or you can follow the well-worn .1-mile path that runs along the shore toward the inlet at the northwestern end of the lake. The trail runs over wide, flat waterside ledges that are ideal for resting, sunning, picnicking and view gazing. Then it reenters the woods and rejoins the carriage road just east of the inlet. From there you can take a left and follow the road back to your car.

6 Bubble Pond

This very easy and dramatic 1.6-mile round trip follows a nearly level carriage road along the shore of Bubble Pond, which lies at the bottom of a long, narrow gorge. It provides uninterrupted views of the pond and the precipitous slopes of Cadillac and Pemetic mountains, which rise steeply from its shores. You'll also see surging cascades and a placid, gardenlike pool in the pond's outlet.

Like all carriage roads, this route is used by bicyclists. Remember to keep alert for them when they pass.

The Walk begins at the Bubble Pond parking area, on the east side of the Park Loop Road, about 2.5 miles south of the intersection of the Loop Road and Route 233 and about 2.5 miles north of the Jordan Pond parking area.

From the southern end of the parking lot, follow the short asphalt path that curves down to the northern tip of the pond. Here you'll have a dramatic view: On your left, the steep side of Cadillac Mountain (Walks No. 19 and 20) plunges into the pond's east shore. On your right, the even steeper slope of Pemetic Mountain (Walk No. 14) rises abruptly from the west shore. Straight ahead, at the southern end of the pond, is the deep, narrow notch formed by both peaks.

Little Long Pond (*Walk No. 8*) *is framed by carefully mowed fields, by the south ridge of* **Penobscot Mountain** (*Walk No. 15*) *and by the top of the* **Bubbles** (*Walks No. 17 and 18*) *(rear). David Rockefeller's boathouse (right) is a focal point.* ▶

After you've savored this view, start walking to your right, along the shore. You'll immediately pass a post marking the Pemetic Mountain Trail.

Keep following the path along the pond. Less than .1 miles from the post the path joins the carriage road, which you'll follow along the entire length of the .7-mile-long tarn.

So close do the slopes of Pemetic Mountain come to the pond that the road has no choice but to hug the water. Sometimes your feet are only inches from the gently lapping waves. So smooth and level is the road, so soothing are the sounds of the pond that the Walk is one of the most relaxing in the park.

As the road ever so gradually bends to the right, past cedars growing on the shore, more and more of the pond slowly comes into view. On your right, through the trees, you can see some of the thousands of rocks that have tumbled down Pemetic Mountain. On your left, across the 500-foot-wide pond, you can see the precipitous lower slopes of Cadillac, so steep that rock slides have covered some of the ledge.

About .7 miles from the parking area, near the southern end of the pond, the road starts to climb away from the tarn. At this point look for an un-marked path on the left that takes you along the pond's flat, grassy southern shore. Start following the path and you'll quickly cross several tiny brooks flowing into the pond. Soon after that you'll have a close view of the pink granite boulders in a large landslide on the eastern shore. You'll also see a dramatic view up the pond: the ledges and cliffs of the almost-vertical-looking slope of Pemetic Mountain on the left, the steep face of Cadillac on the right and, in

between, the low notch between the tw[...]
the northern end of the tarn.

When you're ready, turn around a[...]
toward the parking area. When you reach the nortn-
ern end of the pond, keep walking toward Cadillac
Mountain and you'll immediately come to the outlet
of the tarn — at this point a long, placid, gardenlike
pool dotted with low, wide, smooth rocks.

Cross the pool on the wooden footbridge and follow the outlet downstream. You'll quickly come to a
handsome dam made of huge granite blocks. The
brook plunges over the dam in a frothy fall, four feet
wide and three feet high. Then it surges between
craggy ledges and rushes down a steep glen before
disappearing under a bridge on the Loop Road.

After you've enjoyed this entertaining water show,
follow the path back to your car. On your way, take
another look at the view from the northern edge of
Bubble Pond.

7 Jordan Pond

Probably the best pond-side Walk in the park
is the undemanding, mostly level 3.6-mile path
that takes you all around the unspoiled 1.3-
mile-long Jordan Pond. The trail is always
close to, if not actually on, the very edge of the
water and the pond is surrounded by the steep
slopes of five different promontories: the twin
peaks of the Bubbles and the long ridges of

Pemetic, Penobscot and Sargent mountains. You'll also have close views of Jordan Cliffs and the rock slide known as the Tumbledown.

Parts of the trail go over rock slides and tree roots. This excursion is still a Great Walk, however, because the rocky and rooty sections are neither long nor strenuous — just slow and sometimes picky — and they're outweighed by the otherwise pleasant trail and fine views.

The Walk begins at the Jordan Pond parking area, which is on the west side of the Park Loop Road, eight miles from the park Visitor Center at Hulls Cove, five miles from Bar Harbor, and just north of Jordan Pond House (see below). The Loop Road has several good views of Jordan Pond and Eagle Lake (Walk No. 5), both of which are below and just to the west of the road.

The trailhead is on the western side of the second (westernmost) parking lot. A trail sign here says the "boat ramp" is straight ahead. Go straight and in about 200 yards you'll come to Jordan Pond.

At the shore you'll see the flat, steep face of Penobscot Mountain (Walk No. 15) directly ahead of you, on the west side of the pond. To your right, at

*A cement urn created by the sculptor Eric Soderholtz is a focal point in the **Thuya Garden** seen on a misty day. The garden and the adjacent **Asticou Terraces** are on Walk No. 9.*

◄

the northern end of the pond, you'll see one of Acadia's most famous views: the twin rounded peaks of the Bubbles (Walks No. 17 and 18). Legend has it that the Bubbles were named by a fellow who thought they reminded him of his girlfriend Bubbles; because this is a family publication, we'll leave it at that. You'll keep seeing these steep, miniature mountains after you take the path to your right, which goes counterclockwise around the pond. From here until the end of the Walk, your directions are the same (and rather what you might expect): *Take a left at every trail junction.*

You'll come to your first junction in less than .2 miles and very soon after that you'll cross a marshy cove on a low stone causeway. On the other side of the causeway the trail splits again (remember: go left).

Now the trail is at its best. It hugs the edge of the pond, so you'll enjoy constant views of the water and the pleasant sound of tiny waves lapping the rocky shore. The path is smooth, and carefully placed rocks and log cribs keep the trail level and your feet dry.

Soon you'll be able to see Jordan Pond House, at the southern end of the pond. On the west side you can see the rock slide known as the Tumbledown on the slope of Penobscot Mountain and the carriage road that runs through it. Above the Tumbledown are Jordan Cliffs.

After slightly more than a mile of easy walking you'll come to yet another intersection. Then you'll pass under the steep slopes and cliffs of the Bubbles, on your right. The young white birches here are lovely (but watch out for poison ivy on your right).

Next the trail crosses a rock slide. For the easiest passage, step carefully from one rock to another.

Then, to the right of Penobscot Mountain, you'll see the steep slope of Sargent Mountain (Walk No. 16) rising from the northwestern edge of the pond. (Keep an eye out for another patch of poison ivy on your left.)

In a few minutes more you'll be at the pond's northernmost point. After passing another trail junction (keep left, as usual), turn around for a view of the evergreen-festooned rock cliffs of the Bubbles on your left and behind you, and the steep slopes of Penobscot and Sargent mountains on your right.

The trail then passes a long beach and crosses a marshy cove on handsome log bridges. Look for the beaver lodge on your right.

After reaching the west side of the pond you'll pass yet another trail junction (keep left). On the opposite side of the pond you'll see the Bubbles. To the right of the Bubbles and above the Loop Road are the cliffs of Pemetic Mountain (Walk No. 14).

Now the trail becomes less easy. First it will be rocky in places, then it will cross the rocks of the Tumbledown. As you cross the rocks, look to your right, high above the carriage road, and you'll see Jordan Cliffs.

After passing better and better views of the Bubbles rising dramatically out of the pond, the trail runs through a shady grove of young and old spruce trees. You'll be stepping over roots here for a bit but soon you'll be walking on a smooth boardwalk made of parallel pairs of split logs, flat sides up. The boardwalk will take you over both roots and wet areas almost all the way back to the southern end of the pond.

After rounding a bend, you'll see the gray Jordan Pond House on a small hill.

In a few more minutes you'll pass a concrete dam and spillway on the southern end of the pond. Here the trail crosses a carriage road. Take a left on the road and cross an imposing stone-arch bridge over the spillway, which is the beginning of Jordan Stream. (As on all carriage roads, keep an eye out for bicyclists.) On the other side of the bridge, follow the path that leaves the carriage road on the left and curves along the south shore of the pond. You'll have another view of the Bubbles on your left and you'll see Jordan Pond House on your right. In another couple of hundred feet ahead the path returns to the boat ramp, where the Walk began.

Travel Tip: Instead of returning to your starting point, walk up to Jordan Pond House and, depending on the time of day, enjoy either lunch, "afternoon tea" or dinner at one of the island's best restaurants. Afternoon tea—which, like all Jordan Pond House meals, features its renowned trademark hot popovers—is served on green-topped wooden tables on the lawn, where you can enjoy the classic view of the pond and the Bubbles behind it. A National Park concession operated by the Acadia Corporation, Jordan Pond House also has public restrooms, a snack shop and an excellent gift shop.

8 Little Long Pond

This very easy one-mile round trip, over an

unusually pleasant, wide grassy path, offers a look at landscaping in the grand manner. You can also visit David Rockefeller's boathouse and picnic on the mowed fields beside the pond.

Little Long Pond is on the north side of Route 3 in Seal Harbor, exactly .7 miles west of the intersection of Route 3 and the park road to Jordan Pond. The pond isn't marked but you can see it from Route 3. It's separated from Bracy Cove by a narrow neck of land that's traversed by Route 3 and by a stone seawall on the south side of the highway. There's no parking area—you have to park beside the road.

Seen from the highway, the pond site is a lovely pastoral composition. In the center is the .6-mile-long pond, its long axis perpendicular to the road and its shoreline accented by reeds and trees as it undulates into the distance. The pond is framed by mowed fields sloping down to the water. Surrounding the fields are dark green forests. In the distance, looming over the entire scene, are, from left to right, the southern slope of Penobscot Mountain (Walk No. 15), the two smaller round humps of the Bubbles (Walks No. 17 and 18) and the equally curvy southern ridge of Pemetic Mountain (Walk No. 14). Tucked into the eastern shore of the pond is a focal point: Rockefeller's simple brown-shingled boathouse.

On the north side of the road, near the southwest corner of the pond, you'll see a row of widely spaced boulders beside the road. On the other side of the rocks is a wide path. Start following the path and you'll quickly come to a red-and-white painted metal sign. The sign omits the name Rockefeller, saying instead that the "owner" has allowed public access to the property only for quiet sorts of recreation (such as walking) and that camping, fires and noisier means of transportation are prohibited without his consent. The Rockefellers, who donated about a third of what is now Acadia National Park, no longer use the property and are happy to have the public benefit from it instead. David Rockefeller is preserving the character of the site by maintaining the boathouse and by keeping the fields mowed.

From the sign you can see a carriage path on your left, one of many built by David Rockefeller's father, John D., Jr. Notice its substantial granite abutment and imagine how much money John D. must have lavished on the more than 50 miles of these roads.

You may also see a path leading toward the western shore of the pond. Don't take either the path or the carriage road to the left. Instead, follow the carriage road across the southern end of the pond (parallel to Route 3), then follow a grassy path curving to the left, through the field along the southeastern shore. The path quickly joins a grassy road, which soon takes you to the boathouse.

The doors are locked but you can peer through the windows at the changing rooms and the small, well-built wooden rowboat inside. Gaze over the pond at the fields and forests beyond and at the small beaches on both sides of the boathouse and imagine: You're walking on the Rockefellers' private porch beside their private pond. In fact, you're welcome to do exactly that and to picnic as well. Just be sure to clean up when you're done. Little Long Pond is little known (except by people who've lived in the area for a while) so you'll usually find hardly anyone here. On some days you'll be all alone and it will be *your* private beach and picnic spot.

You can follow the smooth, level, mown-grass road for another quarter-mile before it ends at a carriage road. The pond will be close on your left and the woods will be on your right as you enjoy one of the softest, gentlest paths on all of Mount Desert Island.

When you reach the carriage road, turn around and retrace your steps to your car.

9 The Asticou Terraces & the Thuya Garden

This easy mile-long round trip takes you to two adjacent but very different works of landscape design: the naturalistic Asticou Terraces, created by the Boston landscape architect Joseph Henry Curtis, and the Thuya Garden, designed by the businessman and talented amateur landscape designer Charles K. Savage.

The Walk begins on Route 3 in Northeast Harbor, less than .5 miles southeast of the junction of Route 3 and Route 3 and 198. A red-lettered sign marks a parking lot on the west (ocean) side of Route 3. On the other side of the road a discreet carved wood-and-stone sign says "Asticou Terraces." The sign marks the beginning of a very smooth stone-and-gravel path that gently switches back and forth 100 feet up the steep slope of the spruce-forested hillside.

The Terraces are a near masterpiece of naturalistic landscaping, moving in both their simplicity and their subtlety. The simplicity results from the use of just a few materials: granite stones for the steps and paths, native shrubs such as blueberries and sheep laurel for understory plants and spruce trees for the rest. The Terraces are subtle not only because all the materials are natural to the site but, more important, because the line between the natural and the man-made is invisible. You may wonder: Was the site originally all spruce? It could easily have been. Or did Curtis have to take out some other species to create the unity of the tree monoculture? Were these ferns here or did Curtis move them? On some pavings you're not sure which stones were already in place, which are part of the ledge and which were added. So delicate were Curtis's additions that it's hard to tell. The Terraces are woodland landscaping at its best: not the creation of a garden from scratch but the subtle amending of an existing natural site to improve it, transforming it from mere woods into a woodland garden.

You'll barely start your walk when you'll see a path on your left marked by a sign saying "Curtis Memorial." The path takes you to a 30-by-60-foot oval terrace paved with granite fieldstones and ringed with blueberries and sheep laurel. On the ocean side of the terrace you can see the sailboat-filled Northeast Harbor. On your left, on the face of a 20-foot-high cliff, is a bronze memorial to Curtis, with his bearded profile in relief and the notation that these terraces "are his gift for the quiet recreation of the people of this town and their summer guests."

Walking past the memorial, take a left at two intersections and you'll quickly climb to a handsome fieldstone gazebo. Inside you'll find three rustic wooden benches from which you can enjoy a view of Northeast Harbor. Like everything else on the Terraces, the gazebo honors the principle of unity in design. It blends into its site because it's made of the same granite fieldstones as the paths leading to it, and its pleasing hip roof appears to be made of the same wood as the benches beneath it. The gazebo also honors Frank Lloyd Wright's commandment that a building be not only *on* a site but *of* it.

Retrace your steps to where you took your second left and continue straight ahead. The path quickly takes you to a smaller, rustic, all-wood gazebo near the crest of the hill, which also overlooks the harbor.

From here the path leads you over a charming, moss-banked streamlet on a low rock bridge, over gray granite ledges, past juniper and blueberry bushes, then over a series of low steps made of wooden cribs filled with crushed pink granite. Behind you, through the trees, you'll have more views of Northeast Harbor.

The path ends at Thuya Lodge, Joseph Curtis's blue-gray, wood-framed summer home. (Thuya is the phonetic spelling of *thuja,* the scientific name for cedar, which grows abundantly on Mount Desert Island.) Like the Terraces and the Thuya Garden, the Lodge is now the property of the town of Mount

Desert. Inside you'll find a large horticultural library, a bathroom and a solicitous guide who'll cheerfully answer your questions. The building is open July 1 through Labor Day. Admission is free.

The Thuya Garden, which is open July through September, is next to the Lodge. Unlike the Terraces, the one-acre garden is rather formal: a rolling, well-manicured lawn is the setting for large, straight-sided beds of mostly perennial flowers. Along the edges of the garden, which is surrounded by forest, are informal settings of trees, shrubs and shade-loving ground covers.

After you've toured the garden, retrace your steps down the Terraces and back to your car. For the shortest route stay left at all trail intersections: don't go right to the gazebos or the Curtis Memorial.

If, perchance, you'd like to *drive* to the Thuya Garden, head south on Route 3 from the Terraces parking area and take the first road on your left, about .2 miles from the parking area. The road will bring you to the Thuya Lodge in about .3 miles.

10 The Asticou Azalea Garden

This quarter-mile stroll — easily the shortest, gentlest Great Walk on Mount Desert Island — follows smooth, level paths through a well-designed 2.3-acre naturalistic garden. The paths wind along and across a brook, past Japanese-style sand gardens, around a wide pond, beneath evergreen trees and through about 50 varieties of azaleas, 20 types of rhododendrons, a large number of ferns and mosses, and other trees, shrubs and ground covers.

The garden entrance is about 100 yards north of the intersection of Route 3 and Route 3 and 198 in Northeast Harbor, and about .5 miles from the Asticou Terraces and the Thuya Garden (Walk No. 9). You can see the garden on the north side of Route 3.

Although Charles K. Savage designed both the Thuya Garden and this one, the two designs are quite different. Unlike the more formal Thuya Garden, the Azalea Garden has no flowerbeds and very little lawn.

The azaleas and rhododendrons in the garden were taken from Reef Point in Bar Harbor, the former estate of the landscape architect Beatrix Farrand. The Azalea Garden began in the mid-1950s when, with financial help from John D. Rockefeller, Jr., Savage acquired and graded the site, purchased the shrubs and replanted them here.

Today the garden is maintained by the Island Foundation. It's open during daylight hours from April 1 to October 1 and admission is free. Many of its species are discreetly labeled and knowledgeable guides can answer your questions.

The best time to see the azaleas bloom is usually the last two weeks of June. The peak rhododendron and mountain laurel bloom is usually in early July.

Travel Tip: The Azalea Garden is only about 200 feet west of the Asticou Inn, on Route 3. The inn

...ppointed turn-of-the-century accommoda-
...de even more elegant by its age. The Asticou
a... which provides a fine view of Northeast Harbor, is a good place for an alfresco lunch, a la carte or
a well-presented buffet complete with squid salad
and opulent desserts.

11 Gorham Mountain

This undemanding 1.8-mile round trip is the
quickest and easiest way to see how glorious an
Acadian mountain walk can be. After just a few
minutes of gentle walking, you'll reach open
ledges, where you'll have close, continuous
views of the southeastern coast of Mount Desert
Island. You'll see Otter Cove and Otter Cliffs
on Otter Point, Western Point, the Cranberry
Isles, Sand Beach, Great Head, Newport Cove,
Old Soaker, Frenchman Bay, Schoodic Peninsula, the Egg Rock lighthouse, Schooner Head,
Otter Creek, the Tarn, the Beehive, Huguenot
Head and Cadillac, Dorr and Champlain
mountains.

The Walk begins in the southwest corner of the
Gorham Mountain parking area, which is on the
right (west) side of the one-way Park Loop Road,
about one mile south of Sand Beach and about five
miles south of the intersection of the Loop Road and
Route 3 south of Bar Harbor.

The trail climbs gently past white birches and low spruces and pitch pines and over smooth ledges ringed with blueberry, sheep laurel and bayberry bushes. Some of these ledges are as pretty as rock gardens.

Less than .2 miles from the trailhead you'll start glimpsing the ocean through the trees on your right.

A few hundred feet farther the trail reaches a huge pink granite boulder. Attached to the rock is a handsome bronze plaque saying: "Waldron Bates/pathmaker/1856-1909." The plaque honors the man who built many of Mount Desert Island's trails.

At this point the trail splits. The right fork goes to the bottom of Cadillac Cliffs, on the east slope of the mountain (a rough trail with no views). The left fork heads to the summit.

Go left. Almost immediately after the trail junction, and only a few minutes from the trailhead, you'll reach open ledges with wide views. To the south is Otter Cove (Walk No. 3). On the west side of the cove is Western Point; on the east side is Otter Point. Farther to the south, across Eastern Way, are the Cranberry Isles. To the east is the broad Frenchman Bay.

Walk just a few feet more and you'll see Schoodic Peninsula across Frenchman Bay and more of the ocean behind you. Then, on your right, you'll see Sand Beach and, to the right of the beach, the ledge-tipped peninsula of Great Head (Walk No. 4). Beyond Great Head, in Frenchman Bay, is the orange-and-white lighthouse on Egg Rock.

A few feet ahead you'll see the rock island known as Old Soaker in the mouth of Newport Cove. Behind Old Soaker is the water tower on Schoodic Peninsula. To your rear are Otter Cliffs on the east side of Otter Point (Walk No. 3).

The trail now runs along the top of Cadillac Cliffs. You're about 400 feet above the ocean but less than 1,500 feet from it and you have a 180-degree view — from Otter Point to upper Frenchman Bay. You also have near-bird's-eye vistas of the sea undulating in and out of an unspoiled spruce-and-rock covered coast. You can hear the ringing of the bell on the green buoy off Otter Point and you can see flocks of eider ducks riding the swells. Ahead of you is Gorham's ledgy summit.

About .5 miles from the trailhead, the path to Cadillac Cliffs returns to the Gorham Mountain trail on your right. Go straight ahead toward the summit.

In another .1 miles you'll climb up a ledge with another ocean view. Now you'll see the ocean on both sides of Otter Point and the low Cranberry Isles beyond it. On your left you'll have your first look at the long south ridge of Cadillac Mountain (Walk No. 20).

As you climb farther up the wide, open ledge your views get better and better. In the valley between Gorham and Cadillac mountains, on your left, you'll see houses in the village of Otter Creek. Above the village, on the steep east face of Cadillac, is the cliff known as Eagles Crag. To the right of Cadillac is the lower, 1,270-foot Dorr Mountain, the island's third-highest peak. On your right you'll see surf crashing against the ledges on the east side of the Loop Road, almost 500 feet below. Behind you are Cadillac

Cliffs. In the south, to the right of Otter Point, you again see Otter Cove.

As you climb easily toward the summit, past shrub-size evergreens, you'll see the ledgy hump of the 520-foot Beehive rising just to the left of Frenchman Bay. To the left of the Beehive is the south ridge of 1,058-foot Champlain Mountain (Walk No. 12). To the right of the Beehive are large, handsome houses on Schooner Head (which is outside the park) and surf crashing against the rocky point. You'll also have a 200-degree ocean view, stretching from the west, to the Cranberry Isles, to the northern reaches of Frenchman Bay.

About .9 miles from the trailhead you'll reach the summit. Except for blueberry bushes and low evergreens, it's a bare, flat ledge with views in every direction. Now you can see the triple-arch bridge over Otter Cove and the tiny pond known as the Tarn in the long valley between Dorr and Champlain mountains. To the right of the Tarn, 731-foot Huguenot Head peeks above the western slope of Champlain.

Walk past the summit and you'll have even closer views of Cadillac, Dorr and Champlain mountains, as well as the creased ledges of the Beehive and the valley to the south of it.

When you're ready, turn around and follow the path back to your car — and enjoy Gorham's remarkable views again as you walk "into" many of them on your way down the mountain.

12
Champlain Mountain

This moderate three-mile round trip up Mount Desert Island's easternmost major summit offers close, almost continuous views of coastal landmarks. You'll see Bar Harbor, Beaver Dam Pond, Frenchman Bay, the Porcupine Islands, the Egg Rock lighthouse, the Thrumcap, Schoodic Peninsula, Great Head, Sand Beach, the Beehive, Otter Point, Otter Cove and Southwest Harbor. You'll also see five mountains—Dorr, Cadillac, Kebo, Gorham and Halfway—as well as Huguenot Head and two little lakes, the Tarn and the Bowl.

Champlain Mountain is named for the man who named Mount Desert Island: the French explorer Samuel de Champlain (see pages 71-72).

The easiest way up its 1,058-foot summit is via the scenic Bear Brook Trail, which gently ascends Champlain's north ridge. The trail begins on the Park Loop Road, about .5 miles east of where it runs under Route 3 about two miles south of downtown Bar Harbor. Almost immediately after going under

The pond's mirror-smooth surface reflects the evergreens in the **Asticou Azalea Garden** *(Walk No. 10).* ►

Route 3 you'll pass the Bear Brook Picnic Area on your left, then Beaver Dam Pond on your right (yes, there usually *is* a beaver dam here — right beside the road). Then, just before an overlook of Frenchman Bay on your left, you'll see the small brown-and-white Bear Brook Trail sign on your right. Park at the overlook, cross the road (keeping an eye out for traffic) and begin the Walk.

The smooth path, marked with blazes and cairns, immediately climbs over sunny granite ledges fringed with low birches and pines. Right away you'll get your first view: the steep, ledgy west slope of 1,270-foot Dorr Mountain, the park's third-highest summit, on your right, and, left of Dorr, the rounded summit of 731-foot Huguenot Head, actually a shoulder of Champlain. Just a little bit farther ahead on the path you'll see Frenchman Bay.

As you climb higher and higher your vistas get better and better. Soon you'll see the rocky, spruce-coated humps of the Porcupine Islands off Bar Harbor (Walk No. 1); then Bar Island; then Schoodic Peninsula, on the other side of Frenchman Bay; then the low, 407-foot Kebo Mountain, to the right of Dorr; Great Meadow, below Dorr and Kebo; Beaver Dam Pond and more and more of Bar Harbor. (The only flaws in this otherwise wonderful view are the boxy beige buildings of the Jackson Laboratories, south of Bar Harbor. Try to look the other way and pretend the buildings aren't there.)

The trail is now very pleasant, alternating between smooth gravel paths and wide, smooth ledges as it passes blueberry bushes, pitch pines and spruces.

Very soon you'll come to a ledgy outcrop, where you have an even better view of the ocean. Now you can see more of both Frenchman Bay and the eastern coast of Mount Desert Island, including Schooner Head, to the south; the lighthouse on Egg Rock; the tiny, grass-topped rock island known as the Thrumcap, just offshore, and dozens of white boats dotting the bay.

About halfway up the mountain you'll reach a trail junction. The left fork goes down the steep eastern side of the mountain. The right fork goes to the summit. Take a right—but before you do, turn around and savor the more-than-200-degree panorama, which ranges from Dorr Mountain on your left to the long, slender Schoodic Peninsula and the low islands around it.

As you gradually ascend the spine of the ridge, you'll be climbing farther and farther above the islands and boats in Frenchman Bay. Soon you'll be able to see right up the middle of Main Street in Bar Harbor.

After passing through birches and pines, you'll emerge on sweeping ledges, bare except for a low decoration of handsome scrub pines, sheep laurel, blueberry bushes and other low shrubs. Large two- and three-foot-high cairns now guide your way. Here you'll have a continuous vista of nearly 270 degrees that extends from the summit of Cadillac Mountain (Walk No. 19), west of Dorr, to the mouth of Frenchman Bay. At least 180 degrees of the view is blue ocean.

About a mile from the Loop Road you reach the bare summit, where the ocean view alone is 270

degrees — from Eastern Bay, on the north side of the island, down the eastern shore of the island, past the mansions on Schooner Head Road, to Southwest Harbor and the long, low islands off the southern coast. To the west is the long green ridge of Cadillac Mountain and the more ledgy slope of Dorr. Look carefully and you can see tiny people on top of Cadillac.

After you've enjoyed this remarkable view, take the trail to the Bowl, which goes along the top of Champlain's south ridge.

As you amble across the long, wide, flat ledge of the ridge, more and more landmarks will come into view. Soon, to the left of the trail and about a mile away, you'll see the bare 546-foot-high rock hump of the Beehive. Left of the Beehive is the peninsula of Great Head (Walk No. 4). Right of the Beehive, and almost straight ahead, is Otter Cove (Walk No. 3). Otter Point is on the left side of the cove, Western Point on the right. Then you'll see 525-foot Gorham Mountain (Walk No. 11), north of Otter Point, and Halfway Mountain, north of Gorham and just to the right of the Beehive.

As you walk farther among the low pitch pines, which turn the ledges into a natural rock garden, you'll also see Sand Beach (Walk No. 4) and the

---

Otter Point seen from **Gorham Mountain** *(Walk No. 11). Otter Cliffs are to the left of the point. Baker Island is in the distance; Little Cranberry Island is to the right. In the fall, blueberry bushes on the sunny ledges are bright red.*

◄

as, grassy banks of the mirror-smooth lagoon behind it.

After passing through more pines, you'll get your first look at the Bowl, a tiny tarn in a hollow between the Beehive and Champlain and Halfway mountains.

Keep following the trail down a small dip and back up to a shoulder of the ridge. Now take a few steps to your right, to the western edge of the ridge, and look north. You'll see up the long, steep pass that separates Dorr and Champlain mountains and the narrow little sheet of water in the bottom of the valley called (appropriately) the Tarn. You'll also see the flanks of Huguenot Head to the right of the Tarn. Now walk to the other (east) side of the ridge and you'll see the Egg Rock lighthouse and Schoodic Peninsula.

By now you've walked about .5 miles from the summit and you've enjoyed the best views Champlain has to offer. Turn around here, retrace your steps to your car and enjoy these remarkable vistas again on your way back.

13 Day Mountain

This undemanding 1.8-mile round trip, up one of Mount Desert Island's lowest mountains, offers sweeping views in every direction. You'll see many landmarks, including the Triad, the Beehive, Jordan Cliffs, Frenchman

Bay, Schoodic Peninsula, the Cranberry Isles, Seal Harbor and Somes Sound, as well as Gorham, Champlain, Cadillac, Pemetic, Penobscot, Cedar Swamp, Norumbega, Eliot and Western mountains.

The Walk begins in a parking area on the south side of Route 3, about a mile east of Seal Harbor and about 1.5 miles west of Otter Creek. The parking area has no sign, but it's on the ocean side of the road, about 50 feet east of the height of land, or divide, on the south slope of Day Mountain. From the parking area you can look east and see the Beehive, on the left, the ridge of Gorham Mountain (Walk No. 11) and the mouth of Frenchman Bay.

The trail is on the north side of the road; it's marked by a wooden post indicating that Day's summit is .8 miles away and that the Champlain Monument is to the right.

Take the 100-foot path to the monument and you'll quickly come to a four-foot-high granite rock set on a wide, blueberry-festooned ledge about 20 feet above Route 3. You can see the ocean, nearly 200 feet below and about half a mile away. A plaque on the rock explains that the monument was created "in honor of Samuel de Champlain," the French explorer "who gave the island its name." Another plaque, on the back of the rock, quotes a passage from Champlain's journal. On September 5, 1604, he wrote that his ship "passed...near an island" that was "very high" and "notched in places, so as to appear from the sea like a range of seven or eight mountains close together. The summits of most of them are bare of trees for they are nothing but rock…. I named it the island of the desert mountains." A third plaque says the memorial was erected by the Seal Harbor Village Improvement Society in 1904—the 300th anniversary of both Champlain's voyage and the naming of *L'Isle de Mont-deserts*, or Mount Desert Island.

When you're ready, walk back to the Day Mountain trail and follow the nearly level, slightly rooty path toward the summit. In a few hundred feet you'll come to a trail junction. The short trail on the left (marked by a sign saying "Icy Hill") comes out on Route 3 just west of the height of land. Keep going straight on the Day Mountain trail, which starts climbing very gently, mostly over smooth ledges.

About .2 miles from Route 3 the path reaches the junction of two broad gravel carriage roads. Go right on the first one you come to (it's perpendicular to the trail). Then take an immediate left onto another, 50-foot-long road, which links the first carriage road to the second. Follow the short road to the second carriage road and take a right. Almost immediately you'll see the trail on the left, about 70 feet from

The four Porcupine Islands in Frenchman Bay seen from the north ridge of **Champlain Mountain** *(Walk No. 12), Mount Desert's closest major summit to the ocean. From left to right: Sheep Porcupine Island, Burnt Porcupine, Bald Porcupine (in front of Burnt Porcupine) and Long Porcupine. The tiny island beyond Long Porcupine, at the righthand edge of the photograph, is Stave Island, which is off Schoodic Peninsula, on the other side of Frenchman Bay.* ►

where the path ended at the first carriage road. Beside the trail is a white birch tree with a diamond-shaped piece of blue metal stuck into it; also attached to the tree is a sign saying "Summit."

The trail continues gently up the mountain. Through the trees on your left you'll have occasional glimpses of Mount Desert Island's island-dotted southern coast.

About .4 miles from Route 3 the trail crosses a carriage road again. (This time the trail goes directly across the road.) Remember what this spot looks like because you'll be walking on the *road* on your way back down the mountain and you'll pick up the trail here to go back to your car. There's no sign by the trail, so you'll have to look for other landmarks.

Now you'll climb up and across handsome broad ledges fringed with blueberry bushes, sheep laurel and low spruces. There are no trees here to block your view so you begin to see mountains to the west and the Beehive, Gorham Mountain and Frenchman Bay to the east.

The vistas widen and deepen with almost every step you take. Gradually you see more and more of Frenchman Bay, then Schoodic Peninsula, on the other side of the bay, then Champlain Mountain (Walk No. 12), to the left of Gorham. Behind you the Cranberry Isles appear and, beyond them, the wide blue sweep of the ocean. Then you can see Seal Harbor, less than a mile away. To your left are long, parallel north-south mountain ridges. The modest 422-foot Eliot Mountain is two miles west of Seal Harbor. On the western horizon is the long massif of 1,071-foot Western Mountain, the park's sixth-highest summit. To the right of Western is 839-foot Beech Mountain (Walk No. 24); note the fire tower near its summit. To the right of Beech Mountain is 1,194-foot Penobscot Mountain (Walk No. 15), the park's fifth-highest peak. Behind Penobscot is 942-foot Cedar Swamp Mountain; behind Cedar Swamp is 852-foot Norumbega (Walk No. 32). Beyond Norumbega is Somes Sound.

About .6 miles from Route 3 the trail again crosses a carriage road and then runs across more ledges. Now you have a 180-degree ocean view—from Frenchman Bay in the east to the mouth of Somes Sound in the west and the archipelago of low, sprawling offshore islands in between. You can also see the mountains in the west.

Then the trail goes into the woods and climbs briefly up to the carriage road that curves around the top of Day. Cross the road and walk up to the post in the middle of the ledgy summit, where you'll have a 130-degree view of mountains and a 70-degree vista of the ocean. In the heart of the mountain panorama are three summits dramatically separated by deep valleys. To the northwest is the long, high ridge of Penobscot Mountain; on its steep eastern slope are Jordan Cliffs. East of Penobscot and almost 1,000 feet below its summit is the long valley of Jordan Stream, which flows from Jordan Pond (Walk No. 7) to Little Long Pond (Walk No. 8). Rising from the valley are the ledgy summits of the Triad, almost 700 feet high and less than a mile away. Immediately behind the Triad is 1,247-foot Pemetic Mountain (Walk No. 14), the park's fourth-highest mountain. Right of the Triad is the long valley of Hunters

Brook. To the right of the valley is the southern ridge of Cadillac Mountain (Walk No. 20). Farther to the east is Champlain Mountain. On the western horizon is (appropriately) Western Mountain. To the south are Seal Harbor and the offshore islands.

After savoring this view, follow the carriage road around the east side of the mountain. (Remember to stay alert for bicycles whizzing by.) Here the road is a corniche curving along the top of the cliffs known as The Cleft. As you stroll easily along the wide, smooth, almost level road, you'll have continuous views to your left. You'll see, from left to right: Champlain Mountain, the Beehive, Gorham Mountain, Schoodic Peninsula across Frenchman Bay and the Cranberry Isles to the south.

The road curves around the south slope of the mountain, crosses the trail you walked on earlier, then winds along the west side of the mountain. Now, on your left, you'll see houses in Seal Harbor, islands to the south and mountains to the west.

Then the road switches back to the left and you'll have more views of ocean and mountains through the trees on your right.

Next the trail curves back around the south slope of the mountain and, about .5 miles from the summit, crosses the trail again. From here you follow the path back to your car. If you happen to miss the trail when you come by, don't worry. Just follow the

---

The archipelago of low, sprawling offshore islands seen from ledges on **Pemetic Mountain** *(Walk No. 14) in the fall. Note the bright red blueberry bushes in the foreground.* ▶

carriage road to the next trail crossing—the one where two carriage roads join—pick up the trail there and follow it back down the mountain.

14 Pemetic Mountain

This moderate 3.2-mile round trip to the top of Mount Desert Island's fourth-highest peak offers continuing views of more than two dozen Acadian landmarks, including Schoodic Peninsula, Frenchman Bay, Eastern Bay, Otter Point, Otter Cove, Seal Harbor, Northeast Harbor, Southwest Harbor, the Cranberry Isles, the mouth of Somes Sound, Little Long Pond, Jordan Pond, Jordan Cliffs, Eagle Lake, the Bubbles, the Triad, and Cadillac, Champlain, Day, Norumbega, Penobscot and Sargent mountains.

Although this Walk is the gentlest and most scenic ascent of Pemetic, the middle part of the trail requires some steep climbing over rocks and ledges. This outing is nevertheless a Great Walk because the climbs are brief and the extraordinary views are more than worth the effort.

The Walk begins in a parking area on the west side of the Park Loop Road, about .5 miles north of Jordan Pond House and about 4.8 miles south of the junction of the Loop Road and Route 233, west of Bar Harbor.

The trail is across the road, beside a rushing brook. A post between the brook and the trail indicates that the summit of Pemetic Mountain is 1.6 miles away.

The path follows the brook briefly upstream, then crosses it on a wooden bridge and climbs almost imperceptibly through a damp, moss-carpeted evergreen forest. As you gradually ascend the lower slope of the mountain you'll hear, and occasionally glimpse, another brook on your right.

About .2 miles from the trailhead, near low ledges to the right of the path, you'll reach a trail junction. The path to the Triad goes straight ahead; the trail up Pemetic makes a sharp left. Go left.

The trail now climbs more steeply, sometimes over sunny ledges and sometimes over rocks and the roots of evergreen.

About .3 miles from the trailhead you'll climb up a steep rock outcrop and get your first views: the Cranberry Isles to the south and, through the trees, Jordan Pond (Walk No. 7), Jordan Pond House and Jordan Cliffs on the eastern slope of Penobscot Mountain (Walk No. 15).

The views get broader as you climb. Look behind you and you'll see, from left to right, Seal Harbor, the fields around Little Long Pond (Walk No. 8) and Northeast Harbor. Then, through the trees on your right, you'll see the wooded slopes of the 698-foot Triad, less than half a mile away, and the south ridge of Cadillac Mountain (Walk No. 20) beyond it.

The trail curves to the right side of Pemetic's

north-south ridge and you'll have another view to the east. On the horizon is the long, ledgy ridge of Cadillac; in front of Cadillac is the Triad; to the right of the Triad, and less than 1.5 miles away, is the bare summit of Day Mountain (Walk No. 13).

The trail then descends briefly into a spruce grove and climbs up another ledge. Here you can see Jordan Pond, Jordan Pond House, Southwest Harbor and the mouth of Somes Sound, Norumbega Mountain (Walk No. 32), on the east side of the sound, and the bare top of Penobscot Mountain.

At the top of the next ledge you'll be able to see the carriage road on top of Day Mountain. You'll also have your first view of Little Long Pond and the valley of Jordan Stream, which flows from Jordan Pond to Little Long Pond. Here, too, the Cranberry Isles will be in full view. Sutton Island is the long island, closest to the shore, Great Cranberry Island is beyond Sutton and Little Cranberry is to the left of Great Cranberry. Closer to the shore is Bear Island.

Now the trail levels off and, about a mile from the trailhead, emerges onto a very broad sloping ledge. In a few yards you'll come to another trail junction, marked by a wooden sign in a cairn. The right path

---

The view from the wide ledges on **Penobscot Mountain** *(Walks No. 15 and 16):* **Little Long Pond** *(Walk No. 8) and the narrow causeway separating it from the ocean. Sutton Island is the long island nearest shore; Little Cranberry Island is on the left; Great Cranberry Island is on the right, beyond Sutton Island.*
◄

goes to the Triad, the left to the top of Pemetic. (The sign is incorrect — the summit is about .6 miles away, not .9.)

The junction marks a fundamental change in the Walk. From here to the summit there are virtually no more large trees, only tiny, wind-battered spruces scattered across the wide ledges. From now on your views are continuous.

At the junction you already have a 180-degree vista. On the horizon, but less than a mile away, is the long, steep, mostly bare ridge of Cadillac. To the northeast is a notch in the ridge where the exquisite pond known as the Featherbed is found (see Walk No. 20). Between Pemetic and Cadillac is the long, deep valley drained by Hunters Brook and the tributaries of Bubble Pond (Walk No. 6). To the right of Cadillac is Otter Point (Walk No. 3). To the right of Otter Point is the Triad. South of the Triad is Day Mountain.

Watch for blazes and cairns as you follow the trail up windswept ledges. On your left you'll see Penobscot Mountain again, as well as 1,373-foot Sargent Mountain (Walk No. 16), the park's second-highest peak, to the right of Penobscot, and 1,071-foot Western Mountain on the horizon behind it. Then you'll start seeing Otter Cove to the right of Otter Point, then Champlain Mountain (Walk No. 12) through the notch on Cadillac and Schoodic Peninsula over Cadillac's south ridge.

The trail crosses a tiny stream trickling down from a cedar swamp in a depression to the right of the trail. Then the path curves to the left of the ridge, where you'll have another view of Jordan Pond, now more than 1,000 feet below you but less than half a mile away. Walk a bit to the left of the trail and you'll also see the carriage road and the rock slide known as the Tumbledown on the lower slope of Penobscot Mountain, which rises from the west side of Jordan Pond. You'll also see Jordan Pond House, on the southern end of the pond, and you'll have bird's-eye views of the nearly bare tops of the South and North Bubbles (Walks No. 17 and 18), on the northern end of the pond. Farther to your right is the long north ridge of the North Bubble. About 1.5 miles beyond the ridge is Aunt Betty Pond. Seven miles to the north, between Mount Desert Island and the mainland, is Eastern Bay.

By now the trail has nearly leveled off and you're beginning to cross the mountain's rolling, .2-mile-long summit ledge. Soon you'll see the bare top of Conners Nubble (Walk No. 18), to the right of the North Bubble, and Eagle Lake (Walk No. 5), to the right of the Nubble. Hundreds of feet below, between Eagle Lake and Jordan Pond, is the valley known as Jordan Carry.

Less than .2 miles from the top of Pemetic you'll start seeing a tiny "peak" ahead of you. That's the huge cairn built against a quilted boulder on the summit.

When you reach this granite monument you'll be higher than only three other places on the island—the summits of Dorr, Sargent and Cadillac mountains—and, not surprisingly, you'll have panoramic views. To the northeast you'll see tiny cars on the road to the top of Cadillac. Beyond Cadillac you'll see the ridge of Champlain Mountain. To your left you'll have a 180-degree view that runs from the south end of Mount Desert Island to the north: from the offshore islands, to the valley of Jordan Stream, to Jordan Pond and past the Bubbles to Jordan Carry, then to Eagle Lake and Frenchman Bay. To the south you'll have a 180-degree vista of the Atlantic Ocean: from Schoodic Peninsula in the east to Blue Hill Bay in the west. Take time to wander around the summit and savor the views from different spots.

The summit is also a fine place for a long lunch. (If it happens to be too windy for your taste, find the lee side of the summit cairn and take a seat out of the wind.)

When you're ready to return to your car, retrace your steps to the parking area and enjoy the views again from another perspective.

15
Penobscot Mountain

This moderate 3.3-mile round trip takes you gently to the top of Acadia's fifth-highest mountain and provides frequent views of more than two dozen landmarks, including Frenchman Bay, Seal Harbor, Southwest Harbor, Somes Sound, Bear and Greening islands, the Cranberry Isles, Eagle Lake, Jordan Pond, Little Long Pond and Sargent Mountain Pond; Jordan Cliffs, Jordan Stream, the Amphitheater, the Bubbles, Conners Nubble, the Triad and nine different mountains: Acadia, Cadillac, Cedar Swamp, Day, Eliot, Norumbega, Pemetic, St. Sauveur and Sargent.

This Walk also requires a brief (.1-mile) climb up the cliffs on the east side of Penobscot Mountain. In some places you'll be on your hands and knees on the way *up* the mountain and on your hands, knees and fanny on your way *down*. The trip is still a Great Walk, however, because the climb isn't arduous, just slow, and the outstanding views and gentle grades on the rest of the outing far outweigh the extra effort.

Note: The entire route of this Walk is included in the longer Walk No. 16 (Sargent Mountain).

Like Walk No. 7 (Jordan Pond), this Walk begins in the Jordan Pond parking area, on the west side of the Park Loop Road, about .1 miles north of Jordan Pond House and about five miles south of the intersection of the Loop Road and Route 233, west of Bar Harbor.*

*If you want to begin the Walk at Jordan Pond House, follow these directions to the trail: Walk to the lawn next to the public restrooms, which are underneath the gift shop on the back (west) side of Jordan Pond House. Go west, across the lawn, to the woods. At the edge of the woods you'll see a path and a sign beside it saying that the trail leads to the Sargent and Penobscot mountain trails. The path goes down a steep slope via log steps and in about 50 feet reaches the intersection of two carriage roads on the east side of Jordan Stream. Cross the brook on the foot bridge to the right of the intersection.

From the west side of the westernmost parking lot (the one farthest from the Loop Road and closest to the pond), follow the wide path to the boat ramp on Jordan Pond. In about 200 feet you'll come to the pond, where you'll see the steep eastern slope of Penobscot Mountain on the west side of the tarn and the twin peaks of the Bubbles (Walks No. 17 and 18) on the northern end.

Follow the path to the left, along the south shore of the pond. Almost immediately you'll see, on your left, the long clearing in front of Jordan Pond House, covered with blueberry bushes.

After passing the clearing, the path curves to the left, into the woods and away from the pond. About .1 miles from the trailhead it runs into a carriage road just east of where the road crosses Jordan Stream on a handsome stone-arch bridge.

Take a left on the carriage road and follow it along the east bank of Jordan Stream. The stream, the outlet of Jordan Pond, is one of the largest and fastest brooks on Mount Desert Island. (As on all carriage roads, remember to watch out for bicycles going by.)

You'll walk on the carriage road for just a few hundred feet before it intersects another carriage road. Just before the intersection, take a right and cross Jordan Stream on a foot bridge. A signpost to the left of the bridge says the path on the other side of the stream leads to the "Sargent and Penobscot trails."

On the other side of Jordan Stream the path splits. The trail on the right follows Jordan Stream back to Jordan Pond; the other path goes straight ahead to Penobscot and Sargent mountains.

Go straight and follow the trail through evergreen woods. The path is level at first, then climbs gently before descending gradually to a small brook.

Cross the brook (on stones) and start climbing the lower slope of Penobscot Mountain. On your left a tiny stream tumbles down the steep hill parallel to the trail.

Just a couple of hundred feet from the brook (and about .5 miles from Jordan Pond) you'll climb up rock steps to a charming brook, with small rock-bottomed pools, just below another carriage road. Here the trail to Jordan Cliffs goes to the right, the Penobscot-Sargent mountain trail to the left.

Take a left and climb up the stone steps to the carriage road. As you cross the road, look to your left. You'll see Southwest Harbor and the low islands offshore.

Now climb up the stone steps on the other side of the carriage road and begin the slow climb of the cliffs and boulders on the slope of Penobscot Mountain. (Follow the blue blazes on the rocks.) Almost immediately you'll see three peaks behind you: the long ridge of Pemetic Mountain (Walk No. 14), on the west side of Jordan Pond; the Triad, to the right of Pemetic and above Jordan Pond House, and Day Mountain (Walk No. 13), to the right of the Triad.

The well-built trail switches back to the left, then back to the right. Then it runs along a shelf in the ledge, below a 30-foot-high cliff to the left of the path and beside a wooden fence on the top of a cliff to the right. Next you'll cross a short foot bridge over a chasm and get your first view of Jordan Pond.

Then the trail switches back to the left again and

climbs up a crack in the ledge. Here you'll see the South Bubble (Walk No. 17), on the southern end of the pond. As you climb you'll have wider and wider views of the mile-long tarn. Then you'll catch a glimpse of the North Bubble (Walk No. 18).

About .1 miles from the (second) carriage road you'll reach the top of the cliffs. Then the trail ascends a steep slope but soon levels off on a ledge. (Note the ocean and the islands to your left as you climb.) The path then bends to the right to begin its gentle ascent of the wide, open, ledgy ridge of Penobscot. From here to the summit—about .9 miles away—there are no large trees. Your views will be restricted only by the mass of the ridge itself.

Soon you'll have a 270-degree view, sweeping from the North and South Bubbles, in the north; to Pemetic and Day mountains, the Triad, Jordan Pond and Jordan Pond House, in the east; to Little Long Pond (Walk No. 8), less than 1.5 miles behind you; to the mouth of Somes Sound and Southwest Harbor, in the south. So close is Little Long Pond to the ocean that from here it looks like a tiny arm of the sea. Greening Island is off the mouth of Somes Sound. The .2-mile-wide Bear Island is to the left of Greening and the Cranberry Isles are beyond Bear Island.

As you climb the nearly treeless ridge you'll notice the south ridge of Cadillac Mountain (Walk No. 20) in the notch between Pemetic Mountain and the Triad. You'll also spot the Park Loop Road above Jordan Pond and the low (422-foot) Eliot Mountain to the right of Little Long Pond. Then you'll see more of Northeast Harbor, southwest of Eliot

Mountain. If there are clouds in the south and the light is right, the clouds will cast shadows on the ocean that look like low, dark islands.

The trail then curves to the left (west) side of the ridge, where you'll look into the deep gulch known as the Amphitheater. A carriage road curves along the lower slope of 942-foot Cedar Swamp Mountain, which forms the steep west wall of the ravine.

As you climb, more and more landmarks will come into view: Seal Harbor, to the left of Little Long Pond; 1,071-foot Western Mountain, Acadia's sixth-highest summit, on the horizon beyond Cedar Swamp Mountain; the mountains on the mainland (beyond the Bubbles); Acadia, St. Sauveur and Norumbega mountains (Walk Nos. 21, 23 and 32) between Cedar Swamp and Western mountains; and the summit of Cadillac Mountain to the north of Pemetic Mountain.

Then the trail descends slightly, crosses a tiny marsh and resumes its gradual climb. You're now more than 1,000 feet high and your view expands to include Eagle Lake (Walk No. 5) and Frenchman Bay, to the north.

You'll pass a tiny, picturesque 50-foot-long pond to the left of the trail. Then you'll see the ledgy top of Conners Nubble (Walk No. 18) above Eagle Lake and you'll have another view of the Bubbles.

About 1.5 miles from Jordan Stream you'll come to the six-foot-high cairn on Penobscot's summit. From here you can see Sargent Mountain Pond in the spruce trees in the bottom of the draw between Penobscot and Sargent mountains. To the right of Sargent Mountain are Eagle Lake and, in the distance, Frenchman Bay. Enjoy the view and, when you're ready, retrace your steps to your car.

16 Sargent Mountain

This moderate 5.2-mile round trip is a grand tour. It takes you to the top of both Penobscot Mountain and Sargent Mountain—Acadia's second-highest summit—and offers often continuous views of more than 50 Acadian landmarks, including the Porcupine Islands; Eastern, Western, Blue Hill and Frenchman bays; Bear and Greening islands and the Cranberry Isles; Echo and Eagle lakes; Long, Little Long, Jordan, Sargent Mountain and Upper and Lower Hadlock ponds; the towns of Seal Harbor, Northeast Harbor and Southwest Harbor; Schoodic Peninsula, Somes Sound, Jordan Cliffs, Jordan Stream, the Amphitheater, the Bubbles, Conners Nubble, the Triad, Bald and Gilmore peaks and Acadia, Beech, Cadillac, Cedar Swamp, Champlain, Day, Eliot, Norumbega, Parkman, Pemetic, Penobscot, St. Sauveur and Western mountains.

The first 1.6 miles of this Walk follow the route of Walk No. 15 (Penobscot Mountain) and require some climbing over ledges. See page 84 for a description of Walk No. 15 and directions to the trailhead.

When you reach the summit of Penobscot—the destination of Walk No. 15—the trail splits. The righthand path goes down the east side of Penobscot toward the Jordan Cliffs Trail. The lefthand trail goes straight ahead toward Sargent Mountain.

Follow the Sargent Mountain trail down the ledge north of the summit and into the spruces beyond. For the next third of a mile or so you'll have a brief change of scene: Instead of wide, open granite ledges, you'll be walking on dirt paths through thick stands of evergreens.

The path keeps dropping down a rocky, rooty trail and, about .1 miles from the Penobscot summit, reaches another trail junction in the bottom of the narrow, shady ravine between Penobscot and Sargent mountains. The righthand path goes to Jordan Pond; the trail to Sargent Mountain goes straight ahead.

Follow the Sargent Mountain trail up the ledge on the opposite side of the ravine. Almost immediately the path curves to the left and becomes nearly level as it runs along a low shoulder above the draw. On your left, above the ravine, you'll see cliffs on the north slope of Penobscot and, to the right of the mountain, the ocean and the offshore islands to the south.

In another couple of hundred feet you'll reach the south shore of Sargent Mountain Pond, a tiny (100-foot-wide) lake surrounded by spruce trees.

Bending away from the pond, the trail quickly climbs to the top of a ledge with a splendid 120-degree view. On your left you can see cars on the road on Cadillac Mountain (Walks No. 19 and 20). To the right of Cadillac is Pemetic Mountain (Walk No. 14). To the right of Pemetic is Penobscot; look carefully and you'll see the cairn on its very tip. Down the valley between Penobscot Mountain, on the left, and Cedar Swamp Mountain, on the right, are Little Long Pond (Walk No. 8) and Seal Harbor. Offshore are Sutton and Great Cranberry islands. Through the spruces on your right you can see a bit of Southwest Harbor.

At this point the trail splits again. The left fork goes south toward Birch Spring; the right fork heads north toward Sargent Mountain, now less than .9 miles away.

Take the righthand trail, which quickly takes you out of the trees and up the broad, rolling, lichen-covered ledge on Sargent's south slope. Now you're more than 1,100 feet high—higher than the summits of all but five peaks on the island—and you again have continuous unobstructed views in all directions. To your left is the north-south ridge of 852-foot Norumbega Mountain (Walk No. 32), on the east side of Somes Sound. Across the sound are 679-foot St. Sauveur Mountain (Walk No. 23) and, north of St. Sauveur, 681-foot Acadia Mountain (Walk No. 21). Western Mountain is on the horizon. To the right of Norumbega and less than a mile away is a cluster of three summits: 974-foot Bald Mountain, farthest to the left; 941-foot Parkman Mountain, in the middle, and 1,036-foot Gilmore Peak, on the right. About five miles beyond them is Western Bay, which separates Mount Desert Island from the mainland. Straight ahead is the treeless slope of Sargent. On your right are Cadillac and Pemetic mountains and Frenchman Bay behind them. Penobscot rises to your rear.

The trail runs briefly through spruces again, then reemerges on the ledges. Now you can see Upper Hadlock Pond, to your left rear.

About .5 miles from the summit you come to another trail junction. The path on the left goes to Upper Hadlock Pond; the trail to the top of Sargent goes straight ahead. Here you can also see Lower Hadlock Pond, south of Upper Hadlock, as well as Southwest Harbor, Greening Island, off the mouth of Somes Sound, and other islands farther offshore.

Now you walk across almost level ledge. In about .3 miles you'll reach yet another trail junction. The left path goes to Parkman Mountain; the summit of Sargent is .2 miles straight ahead.

When you reach the massive, 7-foot-high, 20-foot-wide cairn at the summit, you're higher than any other place on Mount Desert Island except the top of Cadillac. No wonder the views are awesome! Almost 1,400 feet below you and less than two miles away is the northern end of Somes Sound. You'll see Somes Harbor and Bar Island, in the mouth of the harbor, the white houses in the village of Somesville and several ponds around the village. Beyond the sound is Echo Lake and beyond the lake is Beech Mountain (Walk No. 24). Long Pond (Walk No. 31), the island's largest body of fresh water, is west of Beech Mountain and Western Mountain is on the horizon. You'll also have a 180-degree view—to the west, north and east—of the narrow bays that separate Mount Desert Island from the mainland.

Walk a couple of hundred feet to the east and you'll see Conners Nubble (Walk No. 18) over Eagle Lake (Walk No. 5) and the North and South Bubbles

(Walks No. 17 and 18) to the right of the Nubble. You'll also see the Porcupine Islands in Frenchman Bay.

Take the time to savor these extraordinary views over a long lunch. When you're ready, turn around and enjoy the vistas again as you walk back to your car.

17 The South Bubble

This undemanding one-mile round trip takes you easily to the top of one of Acadia's most photographed promontories, where you'll have close views of lakes and mountains all around you, including Jordan Pond, Echo Lake, the bare eminences of the North Bubble and Conners Nubble and the dramatic steep slopes of Cadillac, Pemetic, Penobscot and Sargent mountains. You'll also see the ocean and the offshore islands and you'll come face to face with the massive Bubble Rock.

The Walk to the South Bubble can be reduced to a .7-mile round trip if you climb it on Walk No. 18 (the North Bubble & Conners Nubble). If you plan to ascend the South Bubble on that Walk, you may want to skip this one.

Walks No. 17 and 18 both begin at the Bubble Rock parking area, on the west side of the Park Loop

Road, about 1.8 miles north of Jordan Pond House and about five miles south of the intersection of the Loop Road and Route 233, west of Bar Harbor. Just south of the parking area, on the west side of the road, is a viewpoint from which you can see Bubble Rock, high up on the South Bubble. The rock appears to rest precariously on the edge of a cliff, ready to tumble over the edge at any moment. A park sign here explains that the boulder is an "erratic," one of many rocks deposited by the glacier that carved Acadia's valleys and Somes Sound thousands of years ago.

Starting in the middle of the west side of the parking lot, the trail climbs gently through a beech grove for a couple of hundred feet, then turns sharply right.

In another 50 feet it crosses another trail. The path to the right goes to the North Bubble and Conners Nubble (Walk No. 18). The South Bubble is straight ahead. Go straight and follow the smooth path as it rises gently up the South Bubble's lower slope.

In another .1 mile or so the trail turns left and immediately starts ascending steps made from rocks in log cribs.

In another 50 feet the steep trail to the North Bubble splits off on the right. Keep going straight up the steps, past young beeches and white birches.

In yet another 50 feet or so the trail levels off. You're now in the saddle, or col, between the North and South Bubbles.

A few yards ahead, the trail divides again. The path straight ahead goes down to Jordan Pond (Walk No. 7). The trail to the left goes to the South Bubble. Take a left and follow the path over ledges toward the summit. As you near the top, look behind you; you'll see the North Bubble and even the wooden sign at its summit. To your left you'll see the north-south ridge of Pemetic Mountain (Walk No. 14). To the left of Pemetic is the north-south ridge of Cadillac (Walks No. 19 and 20). To your right is the steep slope of Sargent Mountain (Walk No. 16). Left of Sargent, on the precipitous face of Penobscot Mountain (Walk No. 15), are Jordan Cliffs.

Very soon you'll reach the South Bubble's broad, nearly bare summit ledge. On your right is a large cairn marking the promontory's highest point. To the north is a 180-degree view that includes, from left to right: Sargent Mountain, the 872-foot North Bubble, 588-foot Conners Nubble, Eagle Lake (Walk No. 5) and Cadillac Mountain.

A couple of hundred feet east of the sign at the summit is Bubble Rock, an 18-foot-long, 10-foot-high boulder resting on the very edge of the ledge. You wonder how many pranksters have tried to push the rock over the cliff—and how much power would be needed even to budge this multiton monolith. Near the rock you can enjoy another northern vista that stretches from the North Bubble to Cadillac Mountain.

Walk back to the trail near the summit of the South Bubble and follow the blue blazes past blueberry bushes and sheep laurel to the southern edge of

---

Jordan Pond *(Walk No. 7) seen from the* **South Bubble** *(Walk No. 17). Jordan Pond House is at the southern end of the pond.* **Penobscot Mountain** *(Walks No. 15 and 16) rises from the pond on the right.* ▶

ge. Here you have one of the South
dest views. Below you is almost all of
At its southern end is Jordan Pond
of the pond, beyond the low valley of
Jordan Stream, is the Atlantic Ocean, with the Cranberry Isles just off shore. The valley is more than two miles long but from here it looks like a tiny neck of flat land between the pond and the sea. To the left of the pond are the steep faces of Cadillac and Pemetic mountains. To the right of the pond, and rising even more sharply, are Penobscot and Sargent mountains. At the edge of the pond and on the lower slope of Penobscot is the rock slide known as the Tumbledown; if you look carefully you can see the carriage road running through it.

Keep following the trail blazes down several tiers of ledge and you'll have even closer views of Jordan Pond. Walk to your right and you'll be able to see the marshes and wooden bridges at the northern end of the pond, as well as Jordan Carry, the low pass that separates the Bubbles from Sargent Mountain.

If it's not too windy the summit is a fine place to tarry awhile before retracing your steps to your car. During much of the first half of your return trip, you'll be walking "into" the views of the evergreen-festooned ledges of the North Bubble. Enjoy them.

18 The North Bubble & Conners Nubble

This moderate three-mile loop takes you

gradually up two bare summits that offer close, dramatic views of Jordan Pond and Echo Lake and Cadillac, Pemetic, Penobscot and Sargent mountains. Farther away you'll see Frenchman Bay, Western Bay and Schoodic Peninsula.

On your return trip you can make an easy ascent of the South Bubble (Walk No. 17).

Like No. 17, this Walk begins at the Bubble Rock parking area, on the west side of the Park Loop Road, about 1.8 miles north of Jordan Pond House and about five miles south of the intersection of Route 233 and the Park Loop Road, west of Bar Harbor.

At first the Walk follows the route of Walk No. 17 (described on page 94). It climbs gently through a beech grove for a couple of hundred feet, then turns sharply right and, in another 50 feet, crosses another path. The trail to the South Bubble goes straight ahead; the path on the right—to Eagle Lake (Walk No. 5)—takes you to the North Bubble and Conners Nubble.

Follow the righthand trail as it descends almost imperceptibly through moist woods and crosses sluggish brooks on wooden bridges or carefully placed rocks. After passing through hemlock groves and ferns the trail crosses a carriage road about .6 miles from the parking area and just a few hundred feet south of Eagle Lake.

Take a left on the carriage road (and, as on all carriage roads, stay alert for bicycles whizzing by). Almost immediately you'll cross a tepid stream that runs into Eagle Lake and you'll see the cliffs of the North Bubble ahead. As the road gently climbs the North Bubble's steep slope, you'll pass cliffs and huge boulders of talus on your left.

You'll walk about .5 miles on the carriage road before it curves left to cross the saddle between the North Bubble and Conners Nubble. At the crest of the saddle, a trail crosses the road. The trail on the left goes to the North Bubble; you'll follow it later. The trail on the right goes to the top of Conners Nubble in less than .2 miles.

Follow the righthand trail through some pleasant birches and quaking aspens. Then climb briefly up to the Nubble's flat, bare summit ledge and *voila!* Suddenly you have a stunning 360-degree view of forest-fringed Eagle Lake, Frenchman Bay and five of the major promontories of Mount Desert Island.

The Nubble is only 588 feet high but it's the highest point between the Bubbles, to the south, and Frenchman Bay, to the northeast. It's also more than 300 feet above, but less than 500 feet from, Eagle Lake, which extends to the north and east. You therefore have a water-filled view to the northeast: You can gaze up the length of the Eagle Lake, over what looks like a very narrow neck of flat land separating the two-mile-long lake from the ocean, and out over Frenchman Bay, which stretches across to

---

Bubble Rock, an 18-foot-long, 10-foot-high glacial "erratic," seems to rest precariously on the edge of the **South Bubble** *(Walk No. 17). The steep slope of* **Pemetic Mountain** *(Walk No. 14) is on the left.* ▶

Schoodic Peninsula. And that's just a part of the vista. Clockwise, from north to south, you see not only Frenchman Bay and Eagle Lake but also the long ridge of Cadillac Mountain (Walks No. 19 and 20), which parallels the eastern shore of the lake, and the northern slopes of Pemetic Mountain (Walk No. 14). Both mountains are less than a mile away. Continuing clockwise, you see, from south to north, the northern slopes of the Bubbles and the long, steep eastern ridge of Sargent Mountain (Walk No. 16) — all less than a mile away — and across the northwestern lowlands of Mount Desert Island to Western Bay and the mainland beyond. Walk around the wide, smooth granite summit, covered with yellow lichen, blueberries and scrub birches, and you'll enjoy even closer views of the lofty peaks around you.

After savoring one of the best views on Mount Desert Island, retrace your steps down the Nubble to the carriage road and take the trail to the North Bubble, on the other side of the road.

The mossy path runs through a grove of young beeches, then climbs briefly through birches and spruces, which get shorter as you climb higher and the ground gets ledgier.

Soon you'll see your first views. Behind you is Conners Nubble, its cliffs plunging into Eagle Lake and its bands of ledge looking like a rough fortress. If the light is right you'll see the wooden marker on its summit. To the right of the Nubble is another water-filled view over Eagle Lake and Frenchman Bay. Farther to the right is Cadillac Mountain.

Soon the trail levels off and you walk from cairn to cairn on smooth, open ledge, past blueberries, sheep laurel and low spruces. Now your views are almost continuous. Soon you'll see Pemetic Mountain across Jordan Carry, the valley on your left. Beyond the Southwest Pass, the valley to your right, is Sargent Mountain, now less than a quarter-mile away.

The trail goes in and out of stands of low trees as it winds gently for more than half a mile toward the top of the North Bubble. The walking here is superb: an effortless stroll from view to view on a high rock perch.

After passing through low birches and spruces the trail suddenly emerges on the 872-foot summit of the North Bubble. Walk farther out on the ledge and enjoy its 300-degree view. On your left you'll see the stone massifs of Cadillac and Pemetic mountains. Ahead is the evergreen-bedecked rock of the South Bubble. Behind the Bubble is Jordan Pond (Walk No. 7) and behind the pond are the ocean and the long, low islands offshore. To your right are the northern end of the pond and the slopes of Sargent Mountain and Penobscot Mountain (Walk No. 15) rising steeply from the west shore.

After enjoying the view, follow the trail down the southern face of the North Bubble. At first the path is steep; but the steep section is brief (less than 500 feet); it's downhill, so it's not tiring; and it passes overlooks with still more views. You'll see everything you saw from the top of the North Bubble plus Eagle Lake and Frenchman Bay to your left.

The trail soon descends to the saddle between the North and South Bubbles and meets the path to the South Bubble, on the right. From here you can ei-

ther climb to the top of the South Bubble — now just about .3 miles away — or retrace the route of Walk No. 17 (the South Bubble) back to your car.

If you want to climb the South Bubble, follow the description on pages 95-98.

If you want to go back to your car, follow the beginning of Walk No. 17 in reverse: Go straight ahead, down a 50-foot flight of steps made of rocks and log cribs. At the foot of the steps the trail turns right and becomes a wide, smooth track through a beech forest. About .1 miles from the intersection of the North and South Bubble trails, you'll cross the path you followed to the carriage road south of Eagle Lake. From there you return to the parking area, just a couple of hundred feet away.

19 Cadillac Mountain Summit

This very easy, quarter-mile paved Walk around Cadillac's summit offers a 270-degree ocean-and-mountain view from the highest

Conners Nubble *(Walk No. 18) rises more than 300 feet above unspoiled* **Eagle Lake** *(Walk No. 5). Frenchman Bay and the mainland are in the distance. The view is from the long, ledgy north ridge of the* **North Bubble** *(Walk No. 18). Note the cairns marking the trail.*
◄

point on Mount Desert Island—indeed, the highest point on the east coast of the Americas between Canada and Rio de Janiero. The panorama sweeps from Southwest Harbor to the northern reaches of Frenchman Bay and includes a view *down* onto the summit of Acadia's third-highest peak, Dorr Mountain.

These views are rivaled by those from the paved road to Cadillac's summit, one of the most scenic drives in the world. From overlooks along the 3.5-mile highway you'll see Bar Island and the Porcupine Islands off Bar Harbor, the lighthouse on Egg Rock, Schoodic Peninsula, Otter Point, Seal Harbor, Little Long Pond, the Cranberry Isles and other offshore islands, Somes Sound, Eagle Lake, Conners Nubble, the Bubbles, the Beehive, and Gorham, Pemetic, Penobscot and Sargent mountains. Some of these vistas are stunning.

The Cadillac Mountain Road begins on the Park Loop Road, on the west side of the mountain, about 3.5 miles south of the park Visitor Center in Hulls Cove and about a mile south of the intersection of the Loop Road and Route 233, west of Bar Harbor.

You drive barely .7 miles up the road before you come to the first overlook, on the left side of the highway. (Be careful driving across the road.) You're 700 feet above sea level here and Frenchman Bay is spread out below you. You can see Bar Island and the Porcupine Islands around Bar Harbor (Walk

No. 1), the lighthouse on Egg Rock and Schoodic Peninsula, on the other side of the bay.

Drive another mile and you'll come to the second overlook, on your right. You're now 1,000 feet above sea level, higher than most other places on the island. More than 700 feet below, but less than a mile away, is the unspoiled, forest-ringed, two-mile-long Eagle Lake (Walk No. 5). From right to left, you can also see Western Bay, which separates the west side of Mount Desert Island from the mainland; Somes Sound; the cliffs of Conners Nubble (Walk No. 18), on the southwestern shore of Eagle Lake; the steep, ledgy slopes of Sargent and Penobscot mountains (Walks No. 15 and 16); the double humps of the Bubbles (Walks No. 17 and 18); the south coast of Mount Desert Island and the north ridge of Pemetic Mountain (Walk No. 14).

Just .2 miles ahead is the third outlook, on your left. Here, 1,100 feet above sea level, you have a 180-degree panorama that sweeps from Western Bay and Mount Desert Narrows—two straits between the island and the mainland—to Schoodic Peninsula in the southeast and includes almost all the islands in Frenchman Bay in between.

A half-mile farther, on the right, is another 180-degree view. You're now more than 1,400 feet above sea level and you can see, from south to north: the Atlantic Ocean off Seal Harbor; Pemetic Mountain and the low valley to the west of it; Penobscot and Sargent mountains; the North and South Bubbles—long ridges from this vantage point—in front of Sargent and Penobscot, respectively; Eagle Lake and

the entire northern tip of the island, including the northern reaches of Frenchman Bay.

In another .3 miles you come to yet another outlook, on the right. Here, 1,460 feet above sea level, you look down Cadillac's two-mile-long south ridge to some prominent coastal landmarks, including, from left to right: Schoodic Peninsula, the ledgy hump of the Beehive, Gorham Mountain (Walk No. 11), tiny, spruce-tipped Otter Point, Seal Harbor and Little Long Pond (Walk No. 8). Farther away is the sprawling archipelago of low, dark green offshore islands. Beyond the islands is the long ocean horizon. To the right of Little Long Pond you can also see Pemetic, Penobscot and Sargent mountains, the Bubbles, the mouth of Somes Sound and, ten miles away, the mainland. It's a view you can contemplate for a long time.

Just a few feet ahead, on the left, is the Blue Hill Overlook. Turn into the parking lot, walk west on the ledge and experience what may be the mountain's most moving vista. From here the Bubbles and Penobscot and Sargent mountains look like a massive gray monolith festooned with evergreens. You're now so high—more than 1,500 feet—that practically everything else you can see—Eagle Lake, the ocean,

---

Jordan Pond (*Walk No. 7*), *almost 600 feet below the* **North Bubble** (*Walk No. 18*). *Jordan Pond House is at the southern end of the pond.* **Little Long Pond** (*Walk No. 8*) *is to the right of the Jordan Pond House. The ocean and the long, low Cranberry Isles are in the distance.*
◄

the offshore islands and the lakes and lowlands between the mountains—seems like a low, flat, delicate, blue-green, land-and-water membrane. The lowland makes the massif look more massive; the massif, in turn, makes everything else look more fragile. On a slightly misty day, the mountains look like a giant, mossy boulder surrounded by a giant cranberry bog.

Your next stop, just a couple of hundred feet away, is Cadillac's 1,530-foot summit. You'll pass a building on your right that houses restrooms and a gift-and-snack shop. About 200 feet beyond it, at the southern edge of the parking area, is the beginning of the paved summit path. About 100 feet to the left of the walkway, two Park Service plaques identify the landmarks you'll look down on. End to end, the nearly level Walk provides an uninterrupted 270-degree view to the north, east and south. The ocean-and-mountain panorama includes, counterclockwise from the southwest: Southwest Harbor, Seal Harbor, the coastal islands, Otter Cove and the arched bridge over it, Otter Point, the Beehive, Schoodic Peninsula, the long, parallel ridges of Dorr and Champlain mountains (Walk No. 12), the Porcupines and other islands in Frenchman Bay, Bar Harbor and the mainland to the north. Dorr's bare, ledgy 1,270-foot summit is less than half a mile away; you'll be able to see the huge cairn holding up its wooden summit post. Dorr is Acadia's third-highest mountain but now it's more than 200 feet below you.

You'll also pass two interesting Park Service signs. One explains Bar Harbor's very social history; the other describes the granite of which much of Mount Desert Island is made.

The path returns to the parking area a couple of hundred feet north of where you began the Walk.

20 South Ridge, Cadillac Mountain

This undemanding two-mile round trip is a stroll along the crest of Cadillac Mountain's long, treeless south ridge. En route you'll have uninterrupted views of Gorham, Pemetic, Penobscot and Sargent mountains and the Bubbles. You'll also see Seal Harbor, Otter Cove, Schoodic Point, the offshore islands, Little Long Pond, the Beehive, the tiny tarn known as the Bowl and the exquisite pond called the Featherbed. Moreover, like Walk No. 19, you reach the trailhead via the Cadillac Mountain Road, which provides multidirectional views as good as those on the Walk.

Cadillac is the only mountain on Mount Desert Island with an auto road to its summit. Thanks to the road, you can drive up Cadillac and walk down. Because you don't have to walk up the mountain, you can avoid its often rough and viewless lower trails, which run through woods. Instead you can walk on a trail with constant views.

This Walk begins in the Blue Hill Overlook, on the Cadillac Mountain Road, just west of the summit. See Walk No. 19 for directions to the turnoff as well as a description of the extraordinary views along the road.

Leave your car in the overlook parking area and walk just a few feet down the road (away from the summit). Almost immediately you'll come to the bend in the road where you can see over Cadillac's two-mile-long south ridge (described on page 109). Watch out for cars as you cross the road and start walking south along the crest of the ledgy ridge, toward any of the cairns marking the path. (You'll see several on the open ledge, especially with binoculars.)

Your view here is continuous. It includes, from left to right, Schoodic Peninsula, on the east side of Frenchman Bay, the rocky hump of the Beehive, Gorham Mountain (Walk No. 11), tiny, spruce-covered Otter Point, Seal Harbor and Little Long Pond (Walk No. 8). Straight ahead are the low, sprawling offshore islands. Sutton Island is closest to the mainland. Little Cranberry Island is beyond Sutton and to the left. Great Cranberry is behind Sutton and to the right. The much smaller Baker Island is on the

The Porcupine Islands in Frenchman Bay are only some of the landmarks you can see from the quarter-mile long summit walk on **Cadillac Mountain** *(Walk No. 19), the highest peak on the eastern shore of the Americas from Canada to Rio de Janeiro.*
◄

left. To the right of Little Long Pond are (from left to right) Pemetic Mountain, Penobscot and Sargent mountains (Walks No. 14-16). In front of Penobscot and Sargent are the twin peaks of the Bubbles (Walks No. 17 and 18). Behind Pemetic is the mouth of Somes Sound.

As you walk easily across the ledge, past blueberries, huckleberries and other low shrubs, Sargent, Penobscot and Pemetic mountains and the Bubbles will look like a single ridge about a mile to your right. As you approach the southern coast of Mount Desert Island, you'll have closer and closer views of the elegant sweep of offshore islands.

About .1 miles from the road you'll come to a trail junction. The righthand path goes down the west side of the mountain to Bubble Pond (Walk No. 6). The lefthand path goes straight ahead, almost due south on the ridge, toward Blackwoods Campground. Keep going straight.

As you gradually descend the ridge you'll have better and better views of the Beehive, the bay of Seal Harbor, the mile-long Otter Cove and the bridge across it. You'll also see, in a line between you and the Beehive, a tiny pond in the hollow to your left. In the same line, just in front of the Beehive, is a larger pond known as the Bowl.

About .7 miles from the summit road, you'll come to a dip, or hollow, in the ridge. Nestled in the hollow about 100 feet below you is the exquisite pond known as the Featherbed, so called because it's filled with tall, soft-looking lime-green rushes.

The path makes a steep but very short descent to the Featherbed. On the shore of the pond you'll come to another trail junction. The trail on the right goes down the west side of the mountain; the path on the left descends the east side; the middle path stays on the crest of the ridge.

Follow the middle path past the Featherbed and back up to the top of the ridge. Soon you'll see a grass- and moss-lined pool, about 50 feet long and six feet wide, nestled elegantly in the solid ledge. You're now about a mile from the road and you've enjoyed the best views on the south ridge. Turn around here and retrace your steps to your car.

21 Acadia Mountain

This moderate two-mile round trip is a dramatic excursion. As you climb the 681-foot summit, your views will get better and better until they climax with a wide vista up and down Somes Sound — the only fjord on the East Coast of the United States — and over the islands off the southern coast of Mount Desert Island. Your views will also include Echo Lake, Valley Peak and six mountains: Beech, Flying, Norumbega, Sargent, St. Sauveur and Western.

The Walk begins in a parking area on the west side of Route 102, about three miles south of the charming village of Somesville. The trail starts on the other side of the road.

The path climbs up a short flight of stone steps, then over granite ledges dotted with cairns and deco-

rated with blueberries, huckleberries and fragrant scrub pines.

In .1 miles the trail forks. The right fork goes up St. Sauveur Mountain (Walk No. 23), the left to the top of Acadia. Go left.

The trail now runs through open spruce and cedar woods and crosses a brook flowing over mossy ledges.

About .1 miles after the trail junction you'll cross a gravel road and, just a few feet farther on, climb up the cleft of a massive ledge. Then you'll walk on a needle-carpeted path, past tall evergreens, and climb through the cleft of another massive ledge.

Now the trail switches back and forth over more ledges and past pitch pines and blueberries growing in the thin, sun-dappled, needle-covered soil. Here, just a few minutes into your Walk, you can turn around and catch your first views of the two-mile-long Echo Lake and the forested hills behind it.

Climb higher, over more ledges, and turn around again to see not only Echo Lake but also the fire tower on Beech Mountain (Walk No. 24), to the left. On the horizon are the steep, forested slopes of 1,071-foot Western Mountain. To the right of the mountain is Blue Hill Bay, the arm of the ocean between Mount Desert Island and the mainland.

As you keep climbing you'll get an even better

Late-afternoon sun blazes on the long ribbons of Echo Lake and Blue Hill Bay (rear), seen from **Acadia Mountain** *(Walk No. 21).*
◄

view of Echo Lake as well as your first glimpses of the mouth of Somes Sound, the offshore islands and white boats dotting the blue ocean.

Then you'll crest the western edge of Acadia's east-west summit ridge. As the trail levels off you'll walk through more of the pleasant, open, ledgy woods so typical of Mount Desert Island mountains and you'll enjoy better and better views of Somes Sound. Behind you lie the long, blue ribbons of Echo Lake and Blue Hill Bay.

Soon you'll reach the nearly bare ledge of Acadia's 681-foot western summit. Here you'll enjoy even longer and broader views of the ocean. Walk a couple of hundred feet to the northern edge of the summit ledge and you'll see the northern end of Somes Sound, the white buildings of Somesville and Somes Harbor. Walk another 100 feet or so to the eastern edge of the ledge and you'll see the steep, north-south ridge of 852-foot Norumbega Mountain (Walk No. 32), which forms the eastern wall of Somes Sound at its narrow midsection. (Acadia Mountain forms the western wall.)

Return to the trail and walk through the low woods on the saddle between Acadia's east and west peaks. In a few minutes the Walk will culminate in one of the best views on the entire island. At the top of the cliffs of Acadia's eastern summit—only 1,500 feet from the sound but nearly 700 feet above it—you'll have a 180-degree view up and down the fjord and out into the Atlantic. You'll see past Northeast Harbor, on the east side of the Sound; Southwest Harbor, south of the Sound; Greening Island, just beyond the Narrows at the mouth of the Sound; and the low, elegant sprawl of a half-dozen other offshore islands. To the right of the islands you can see still another 90 degrees. From left to right, the landmarks are the low (284-foot) Flying Mountain (Walk No. 22), on a point of land near the southwestern end of the Sound; the graceful curve of Valley Cove, on the northern edge of the point; 521-foot Valley Peak and the long ridge of St. Sauveur Mountain (both Walk No. 23); and, far to your right, the fire tower atop 839-foot Beech Mountain. In the summer the blue water below you is dotted with a flotilla of white sailboats.

From this vantage point the long, narrow sound looks more like a blue river than an arm of the ocean. But the steep slope of Norumbega on the opposite shore and the even higher ridge of 1,373-foot Sargent Mountain (Walk No. 16) beyond it are reminders that the Sound is geologically a fjord: a deep, narrow ocean bay carved by glaciers and surrounded by mountains.

This ledgy perch is a superb place for a picnic, or at least a long rest. Whatever you do, take time to appreciate the surpassing panorama before following the trail back to your car.

22 Flying Mountain

This undemanding 1.1-mile loop takes you up Acadia's lowest and gentlest mountain, where you'll enjoy panoramic views of Somes Sound, the mountains around the fjord, and

the south coast of Mount Desert Island. You'll see Fernald Cove, Southwest Harbor, Greening Island, the Cranberry Isles, Northeast Harbor, Valley Cove, Valley Peak and Norumbega, Acadia, St. Sauveur, Beech and Western mountains.

The Walk involves some *very* brief climbing up and down ledges. The trip is still a Great Walk, however, because the climbing is neither difficult nor tedious and it's vastly outweighed by the Walk's many excellent views and otherwise undemanding trail.

The Walk begins at a parking area near the end of Fernald Cove Road, near the mouth of Somes Sound. Fernald Cove Road goes east from Route 102, which runs along the west side of Somes Sound; the intersection is about a mile north of Southwest Harbor and exactly 5.5 miles south of the junction of Route 102 and Route 3 and 198 in Somesville.

The mouth of Somes Sound — the only fjord on the east coast of the United States — seen from the ledges on the eastern summit of **Acadia Mountain** *(Walk No. 21). The bay to the right is Valley Cove. The thickly forested point at the edge of the cove is* **Flying Mountain** *(Walk No. 22). Northeast Harbor is on the left; Southwest Harbor is near the horizon on the right. Greening Island is between Northeast Harbor and Southwest Harbor; Great Cranberry Island is on the horizon to the left.*

◄

Fernald Cove Road crosses the northwestern edge of Fernald Cove about .8 miles from Route 102. Just a few hundred feet past the cove, on the left, is the pleasingly landscaped Valley Cove parking area.

The trail begins at an opening in the stone wall on the east side of the parking area. Walk up the stone steps and follow a rooty trail through spruce woods.

Soon you'll see a trail branching off to the left. Ignore it and keep going straight. You'll climb gently over ledges and quickly see a large mound of ledge looming across the trail. Climb to the top of the ledge (with a couple of assists from your hands and knees) and *voila!* After walking less than ten minutes and less than 1,000 feet, you're at the top of Flying Mountain—and the views are terrific. About 284 feet below you and less than 1,000 feet away is Somes Sound. Directly across the long, narrow fjord, impressive residences dot the grassy eastern shore. Rising to the left of the mansions are the steep slopes of 852-foot Norumbega Mountain (Walk No. 32). To the right are the houses of Northeast Harbor. Farther to the right, in the mouth of the sound, is Greening Island. To the left of Greening and farther away are the low Cranberry Isles. Directly below you on your right, and less than 1,500 feet away, is Fernald Cove. On the south side of the cove is Connor Point. Farther away is Southwest Harbor. Less than 1,000 feet to the west are the cliffs of Valley Peak (Walk No. 23). Beyond Valley Peak is Beech Mountain (Walk No. 24); you can see the fire tower on its summit. On the horizon is 1,071-foot Western Mountain.

The views continue as the trail curves across the

open ledge to the east side of the mountain, bringing you even closer to the sound. Now you can see, directly below, the flat mowed fields along the undulating western shore of the sound north of Fernald Cove.

The trail now climbs off the summit ledge and heads north along the nearly level, ledgy spruce-covered spine of the Flying Mountain ridge.

Less than .2 miles from the summit you reach a junction. The trail to the right, marked by a sign saying "Overlook," takes you, in just a couple of hundred feet, to another ledge above Somes Sound. From here you can see far up the curving walls of the steep-sided fjord. To the left, the nearly vertical face of 681-foot Acadia Mountain (Walk No. 21) springs straight out of the water. On the opposite shore, Norumbega rises even higher.

Go back to the main trail and keep following it to the northern shoulder of Flying Mountain. In just a few feet you'll reach a ledge where you'll have a view, above the spruces, of Valley Peak, on the left; St. Sauveur Mountain (Walk No. 23), to the right of Valley Peak, and Acadia Mountain, straight ahead. Below Acadia Mountain is the cliff-walled bay on the west side of Somes Sound known as Valley Cove.

Then you'll immediately come to another ledge, where the view is even better. You'll see the nearly vertical Eagle Cliffs—among the steepest on the island—on St. Sauveur Mountain as well as sailboats in Valley Cove, Norumbega Mountain to the east and the northern reaches of the five-mile-long Somes Sound.

Now you'll climb down the steep ledge (occasion-

ally on your fanny), then down rough talus through open spruce woods. (This section is brief and not difficult; you just have to take your time negotiating the rocks in the trail.)

Then the trail runs through the spruces and, about .5 miles from the trailhead, reaches the shore of Valley Cove, a small, graceful inlet ringed by mountain walls that look even taller than the cove is wide. Just a few hundred feet away, on the western edge of the cove, is the talus of the rock slide below Eagle Cliffs. Across the cove is Acadia Mountain. Opposite the sound is Norumbega Mountain.

After crossing several brooks running into the cove, you'll walk up log steps and then up a wide, rooty path to a loop at the end of the Valley Cove Road.

Follow the smooth, level, half-mile-long gravel road back to the parking area. As you walk through the spruce woods, you'll have glimpses, through the trees, of the steep slopes of Flying Mountain, on your left, and the cliffs of Valley Peak, on your right.

23 Valley Peak & St. Sauveur Mountain

This moderate 1.4-mile round trip presents a

*The sinuous shore of **Long Pond** (Walk No. 31), Mount Desert Island's largest body of fresh water, seen from **Beech Mountain** (Walk No. 24).*
◀

gallery of vistas of Somes Sound from ledgy overlooks on two different summits near its western shore. You'll see Fernald and Norwood coves, Southwest Harbor, Baker and Greening islands, the Cranberry Isles, Northeast Harbor, Valley Peak (from St. Sauveur), as well as Acadia, Eliot, Day, Norumbega, Penobscot, Sargent and Flying mountains.

The first part of the Walk is a steep, rocky, rooty trail. It's still a Great Walk, however, because the section is only a quarter-mile long—too short to be tedious—and the views easily outweigh the brief inconvenience.

Like Walk No. 22 (Flying Mountain), this excursion begins near the end of Fernald Point Road. To reach the trailhead, follow the directions to Walk No. 22 on page 119. When you reach the Valley Cove parking area, follow the gravel Valley Cove Road, which begins on the north side of the parking area. The Walk begins at the Valley Peak trailhead, which is on the left (west) side of the road, .1 miles beyond the parking area. You can park at the trailhead if there's room; otherwise leave your car at the Valley Cove parking area.

The trail immediately descends through a spruce forest and quickly reaches a brook that flows into Fernald Cove. The rooty path crosses the stream on a log bridge, then recrosses it on stones and another log bridge.

Then the trail becomes rooty *and* rocky as it starts climbing the east slope of Valley Peak, and it gets steeper as it climbs higher up the mountain. Through the trees behind you'll have glimpses of the west slope of Flying Mountain. Then you'll see Somes Sound and Northeast Harbor.

About .3 miles from the trailhead the trail begins to level off. Instead of passing through spruces, it now runs over smooth granite ledges fringed with junipers, low pitch pines and cedars.

As you approach the summit of Valley Peak, your view expands with each step. You'll see Northeast Harbor on the east side of Somes Sound, Southwest Harbor on the west side, Greening Island at the mouth of the sound and the Cranberry Isles beyond. Then you'll see the narrow Fernald Cove, less than a quarter of a mile away, on the west side of the sound, then Bear Island off Northeast Harbor.

About .4 miles from the trailhead you'll reach the summit ledge. Walk to the right of the summit marker—a wooden sign in a cairn—and follow the ledge to the north, parallel to Somes Sound. Here you'll have a 200-degree view of water that stretches from the northern reaches of the sound all the way to Southwest Harbor. The vista includes the long ridge of 1,373-foot Sargent Mountain, the park's second-highest peak, on the horizon on the other side of the sound. In front of Sargent is 852-foot Norumbega Mountain, rising from the east side of the fjord. On the flat shore to the right of Norumbega are a score of large, handsome residences. To the right of the houses you can see, from left to right, Northeast Harbor; Greening Island, in the mouth of the sound, the Cranberry Isles beyond it, and Southwest Harbor, on the other side of the sound. North of South-

west Harbor is Norwood Cove. Directly below is the placid green Fernald Cove. North of the cove is the low, grass-covered Fernald Point; south of the cove is Connor Point.

Follow the path farther along the ledge (it's marked with cairns and blue blazes), then into the woods. You'll soon start climbing gently up St. Sauveur Mountain and catching glimpses of the sound through the trees on your right.

About .2 miles from Valley Peak you'll emerge onto the eastern ledges of St. Sauveur. As you walk north along the clifftop you'll enjoy unobstructed views up and down Somes Sound.

About .3 miles from Valley Peak you'll reach an overlook on the northeast shoulder of St. Sauveur. Now you'll see Acadia Mountain (Walk No. 21) rising out of the deep waters of the sound to your left. You'll also see Day Mountain (Walk No. 13) and Eliot Mountain beyond Northeast Harbor. Directly below, on the curving wall of Valley Cove, are the awesome 600-foot-high Eagle Cliffs. To your right is Valley Peak. Left of the peak is Flying Mountain.

You're now about 650 feet above the sound—high

*Clouds fill Somes Sound and dramatically encircle mountains east of **Beech Mountain** (Walk No. 24). **Sargent Mountain** (Walk No. 16), the second-highest peak on Mount Desert Island, is on the horizon. The precipitous ledgy face of **Acadia Mountain** (Walk No. 21) is on the left. The low, forested ridge of **St. Sauveur Mountain** (Walk No. 23) is on the right.*

◀

enough to see the massive cairns on the summits of
Sargent and Penobscot mountains on the horizon on
the far side of the sound. From this altitude, Northeast Harbor, Southwest Harbor and the offshore
islands look so low and flat that, in a big storm, the
sea might wash right over them.

From here the path heads west, away from the
ledges and toward the summit of St. Sauveur. The
summit, however, has no views at all—let alone one
as spendid as the one you're watching now. So after
you've enjoyed the panorama, follow the trail back to
your car.

24 Beech Mountain

This undemanding 2.2-mile round trip provides lofty but intimate views of Long Pond,
Mount Desert Island's largest lake. It also offers
panoramic views of more than a dozen island
landmarks, including Beech Cliff, Echo Lake,
Somes Sound, Southwest Harbor and the offshore islands, Bartlett Island, Western Bay and
Acadia, St. Sauveur, Flying, Sargent, Norumbega, Cadillac, Day and Western mountains.

The Walk begins in a parking area at the end of
Beech Hill Road, about four miles south of Somesville. To reach the trailhead, turn west off Route 102
about .2 miles south of Higgins' store in the center of
Somesville; there's a park sign at the junction. In

another .2 miles turn left onto Beech Hill Road, which will take you gradually up the long ridge that separates Echo Lake from Long Pond (Walk No. 31). Across mowed fields you'll see mountains on both sides of the road. Straight ahead is the fire tower on Beech Mountain. On your right is 1,071-foot Western Mountain, the sixth-highest summit on Mount Desert Island. On your left is the long north-south ridge of 1,373-foot Sargent Mountain (Walk No. 16), the island's second-highest peak, on the horizon. To the right of Sargent, and almost a mile closer, is another north-south ridge: 852-foot Norumbega Mountain (Walk No. 32). To the right of Norumbega, and closer still, is 681-foot Acadia Mountain (Walk No. 21). Acadia's ridge runs east-west, perpendicular to the road, so from here the mountain looks much more compact than either Norumbega or Sargent.

About 3.5 miles from Higgins' store the paved road dead-ends alongside the parking area, which nestles against cliffs and a large boulder on the lower slope of Beech Mountain. The trail to the summit begins in the northwest corner of the parking lot.

After running along a brook for a couple of hundred feet, the path splits. Both forks will take you to the summit but the righthand trail is gentler and its views are much better. Go right.

The trail is a wide, smooth, gravelly path through a mixed forest. Very soon you'll see Long Pond below on your right, set in the middle of forest. Its thinly developed wooded shoreline (much of which is outside the national park) twists in and out of coves. The long, pointed Northern Neck extends into the center of the pond from the north; the smaller Southern Neck reaches toward the Northern Neck from the west side of the pond. The two peninsulas are only about 700 feet apart; together they almost divide the pond in two.

As you gently climb the mountain, the views of the pond through the trees get better and better and you'll see 480-foot Carter Nubble behind you, on the east side of the pond.

As you near the top of the mountain, you're almost 800 feet above Long Pond but only about 1,500 feet away from it, so you have glorious bird's-eye views. Over low evergreens and ledges thick with blueberries, you can see almost the entire length of the four-mile-long pond. Directly across the water, the steep, ledgy slopes of Western Mountain spring up from the shore. In the distance is the long, narrow Western Bay, which separates Mount Desert Island from the mainland. You'll be able to see this vista almost all the way to the top of the mountain.

Near the summit, the trail intersects two paths that go down to Long Pond. Go straight ahead—i.e., take the left fork—at each junction. Immediately after the intersections you'll climb a flight of log steps. At the top of the steps, look to your right. On top of a wide, bare ledge you'll see a 30-foot-high steel observation tower. It's occasionally manned by national park volunteers.

Sailboats skim across Echo Lake below the 600-foot-high **Beech Cliff** *(Walk No. 25). The forested slopes of* **Acadia Mountain** *(Walk No. 21) rise steeply on the right.* ▶

Climb up the tower and enjoy its 360-degree views of landmarks in the heart of Mount Desert Island. To the northeast you can see Beech Cliff (Walk No. 25) above Echo Lake, as well as Somesville and the northern end of Somes Sound. East of Echo Lake is Acadia Mountain. South of Acadia, and almost due east, is St. Sauveur Mountain (Walk No. 23). South of St. Sauveur is Flying Mountain (Walk No. 22). Behind Acadia is Sargent Mountain and behind St. Sauveur is Norumbega. In the distance, to the right, is the long south ridge of Cadillac Mountain, the park's highest summit (Walks No. 19 and 20). To the right of Cadillac is Day Mountain (Walk No. 13). To the south is Southwest Harbor and Greening Island, off the mouth of Somes Sound. To the southeast are the Cranberry Isles. To the west is the long blue ribbon of Long Pond and, beyond the pond, the steep slopes of Western Mountain. To the northwest are Bartlett Island and Western Bay.

You can also see many of these landmarks from the broad ledge beneath the tower, making it a fine place for lunch.

When you're ready, follow the path back to your car—and enjoy the views of Long Pond again.

25 Beech Cliff
& Canada Cliff

This easy one-mile round trip brings you to

the top of the Beech and Canada cliffs, where you'll have exhilarating bird's-eye views of Echo Lake, more than 500 feet below. You'll also see Acadia, St. Sauveur, Norumbega and Sargent mountains, on the far side of the lake, as well as Somes Sound, Somesville, Southwest Harbor, Greening Island and the Cranberry Isles. No other Walk on Mount Desert Island offers such grand views for so little effort.

Like Walk No. 24, this trip begins in a parking area at the end of Beech Hill Road, about 3.5 miles south of Somesville. See pages 130-131 for a description of the route to the trailhead.

The path to the cliffs begins on the east side of Beech Hill Road, opposite the northeast corner of the parking lot, and rises very gently as it passes through a moist evergreen grove.

In about .3 miles the path crosses two trails: an unmarked path on the left and a trail on the right that goes to Echo Lake. Walk straight ahead. Almost immediately you'll come to the top of Beech Cliff.

Be careful here—there's nothing between you and a long fall but air. Follow the faint path along the top of the cliff. You'll see—and hear—people on the beach in the cove at the southern end of Echo Lake, almost directly below you. You'll also have a bird's-eye view of sailboats tacking back and forth on the two-mile-long lake, more than 500 feet below. Since you're almost on top of the lake, you'll actually be able to see its bottom through the shallow green water near the shore.

On the other side of the lake are the overlapping ridges of four mountains. Rising dramatically from the opposite shore of the lake is St. Sauveur Mountain (Walk No. 23). Beyond and to the left of St. Sauveur is Acadia (Walk No. 21). Behind both Acadia and St. Sauveur is Norumbega (Walk No. 32) and behind both Acadia and Norumbega is Sargent (Walk No. 16). In the distance to the right is Greening Island, in the mouth of Somes Sound; the Cranberry Isles, beyond Greening Island; and Southwest Harbor, to the right of Greening. On your far right is Canada Cliff.

As you walk north along the top of the cliff you'll see the northern end of Echo Lake and, farther away, the village of Somesville and the northern end of Somes Sound.

Soon the path bends away from the cliff and into the woods. Turn around here and walk back to the path to Echo Lake.

Follow the Echo Lake trail for about 300 feet and you'll come to the top of Canada Cliff, which also overlooks Echo Lake. Walk (carefully!) along the edge of the precipice. The view here rivals the one you just saw. The near-vertical Beech Cliff, now on your left, sweeps dramatically up from the lake. On the other side of the long lake are the knitted ridges of St. Sauveur, Acadia, Norumbega and Sargent mountains. Somesville lies off the northern end of the lake; the mouth of Somes Sound is to your right. These views continue until the path curves away from the cliff in another couple of hundred feet and reenters the woods.

The vistas from Beech and Canada cliffs capture

the essence of Mount Desert Island: a landscape made of steep mountains surrounded by some kind of water—a lake, a pond, a fjord or the ocean.

Obviously, these ledges are wonderful picnic spots. Tarry long enough and you'll probably see a bald eagle soaring above the lake.

After enjoying the view, turn around and retrace your steps to your car.

Great Walks of Isle au Haut

See pages 9 and 10 for information on how to get to the island and where to stay.

All four of the island's Great Walks begin at the junction of Western Head Road and the path from the ferry landing. To reach the junction, take a left when you walk off the landing and follow the narrow, evergreen-shaded path along the south shore of Duck Harbor. You'll cross, on large stones, a brook flowing into the harbor and, about .2 miles from the landing, come to Western Head Road. You'll see a picnic table and a portable toilet near the intersection.

The routes of Walks No. 26, 27 and 28 overlap in places. If you take the Walks separately you'll be walking some trails—particularly Western Head Road—at least three times. If you have enough time and energy, you can avoid the repetition by combining parts of two, or even all three Walks in one outing. For example, instead of taking Western Head Road to the Goat Trail (Walk No. 26), you could take either the Cliff and Western Head trails (Walk No. 27) or the Duck Harbor Mountain Trail (Walk No. 29). Or you could take the Cliff and Western Head trails to the Goat Trail and the Duck Harbor Mountain Trail back to Duck Harbor, or vice versa, and thereby do all three Walks in one outing. (That combined Walk, however, would be about 8.2 miles, leaving you little time to linger at beautiful places.) Consult the park map of Isle au Haut and create your own combinations.

26 The Goat Trail

This moderate 6.6-mile round trip is the most exhilarating walk on Isle au Haut and the most exciting *ocean shore* walk in Acadia National Park. It takes you down to the beaches of five often-deserted coves and up bare, wind-blown headlands, where you have continuous bird's-eye vistas of waves crashing against the island's wild and rugged southern coast.

From the intersection of Western Head Road and the trail to the ferry landing, follow the grassy road as it rises gently through a clearing, past blueberry bushes and spruces, and past the trail to Duck Harbor Mountain (Walk No. 29), on the left. After less than a quarter of a mile the road levels off and runs through lush spruce woods. Through the trees on your left you'll see granite cliffs on the lower slopes of Duck Harbor Mountain.

After about 1.3 miles of very pleasant, nearly level walking, you'll reach the Goat Trail, on your left.

Start walking on the Goat Trail and you'll immediately see Deep Cove on your right. You'll also see

---

Ledgy, surf-washed headlands on Isle au Haut, seen from the **Goat Trail** *(Walk No. 26). Eastern Head is in the distance, on the left. In the fall, blueberry bushes (lower right) are bright red.* ▶

surf breaking on tiny rock islands offshore, on the ledge walls of the cove, and on Eastern Head, almost two miles to the east.

The path runs through grassy spruce woods, close to the rocky beach of the cove, and quickly crosses a stream flowing into the ocean.

Then the nearly level trail passes through thick, damp spruce woods until, about .4 miles from Western Head Road, it reaches a junction with the Duck Harbor Mountain Trail at Squeaker Cove. The tiny cove, just a couple of hundred feet wide, is framed by granite cliffs. Waves rush through the rock walls and crash on the rocky beach. The surf grinds the stones against each other, gradually wearing them down, making them smoother and rounder. The "squeaking" sound of rocks scraping against rocks gives the cove its name.

The Goat Trail now climbs quickly back into deep, moss-floored spruce woods and soon approaches a narrow stream rushing into a tiny, 25-foot-wide cove. The trail bends back from the brook and climbs away from the ocean before crossing the creek farther upstream.

Then the trail quickly climbs up to a ledge knob with the best view of the entire Walk. Here you're 100 feet above the ocean—about the highest point on the Goat Trail. Squeaker Cove is directly below and barely a few hundred feet away. The finely textured stony beach at the head of the cove is a pleasant contrast with the solid, massive headlands on either side of it. The concavity of Squeaker Cove is gracefully echoed by Deep Cove, just beyond it, and by another cove farther away. The rock point on the west side of Squeaker Cove is echoed by another point on the west wall of Deep Cove and by Western Head, on the end of the island. This elegant undulating rock sculpture is dramatically defined by a long, unbroken fringe of white surf at its base. High above the surf, north of Squeaker Cove, are the southern ledges of Duck Harbor Mountain.

This vantage point is a pleasant aerie—a sunny, lichen-covered ledge landscaped by nature with low spruces and thick, neat clumps of even lower blueberry bushes. It's perfect for lunch, or at least a long pause.

The bird's-eye vistas continue as the trail curves along the top of more headlands, high above the ocean. Now you'll have 180-degree views of the entire south coast of the island, from Eastern Head to Western Head. You'll see miles of surf crashing against head walls and over tiny rock islands, and flocks of white-and-black eider ducks bobbing on the rocking sea.

Then the path winds down from the headlands and back into the woods. Soon, through the spruces, you'll catch glimpses of Barred (not Bar) Harbor; if the tide isn't too high you'll see the sandbar at its mouth that gives the cove its name. Then the trail curves along the head of the harbor, close to its rocky beach, affording continuous views of the most beautiful cove on the Walk. The two long, elegant arms of the harbor curve like the pincers of a crab, embracing the shallow water of the cove in a graceful circle.

About .9 miles from Squeaker Cove the Median Ridge Trail joins the Goat Trail on the left. Go

straight ahead. Right after the intersection you'll cross a small brook on stones just before it flows into Barred Harbor.

Next the trail curves around the east side of the harbor, where you'll have another view of Western Head. Then it reenters the woods, where you'll have more views of the harbor through the trees on your right.

The path soon emerges on ledges, with a wide view that includes both Eastern and Western heads. Then it crosses a rock beach at the head of a small, unnamed cove. The last time we were here—a bright, windy fall day—the green-tinted blue sea was dotted with white caps and surf was leaping up the ledges below us.

The ocean views continue as the path winds through sunny, grassy spruce woods to the western side of Merchant Cove, a large bay on the west side of Head Harbor. On the opposite shore, about half a mile away, is the long, low, surf-washed peninsula of Eastern Head, the eastern arm of Head Harbor.

The Goat Trail curves along the grassy shore of Merchant Cove, offering uninterrupted views of the cove and Eastern Head. After passing long drifts of beach peas (which look like sweet peas) on the left, you'll reach the head of the cove. The wooden sign identifying the cove is about .6 miles from the Me-

Surf crashes on the rough rocky coast of Isle au Haut, seen from the **Western Head Trail** *(Walk No. 27). In the distance are the Camden Hills, on the mainland.*
◄

dian Ridge Trail and about two miles from Western Head Road.

From here you can return to Duck Harbor in one of three ways: by retracing your route in its entirety (making the Walk a 6.6-mile round trip), by taking the Cliff and Western Head trails (Walk No. 27) or — if you have a lot of time and energy — by taking the Duck Harbor Mountain Trail (Walk No. 29).

27 The Cliff & Western Head Trails

This moderate excursion — 4.3 or 5.2 miles, depending on how you return to the trailhead — is one of the most exciting shore walks in the park. It offers both cliff-top and beachside views of the dramatic coast on both sides of the long point known as Western Head.

Like the other Great Walks on Isle au Haut, this one begins on Western Head Road in Duck Harbor. See the second paragraph of Walk No. 26 on page 140 for a description of the road.

After about .6 miles of easy, pleasant walking on Western Head Road you'll reach the northern end of the Western Head Trail, which joins the road on your right.

The sometimes rooty trail passes through a moist spruce forest and crosses wet areas on boardwalks made of two half-logs placed side by side. The path descends gradually, almost imperceptibly, to the shore.

About a quarter-mile from the road you'll reach a ledgy headland, where you'll have a 180-degree view up and down the rocky west coast of Western Head. The Saddleback Ledge lighthouse is about three miles offshore.

The ocean views continue as the path crosses a stony 200-foot-long beach, traverses a grassy area above a large headland, and crosses one small and one large (300-foot-long) pebbly beach. A tranquil marsh, protected from the sea by a rock berm, lies just to the left of the second beach.

Then the trail goes through a short tunnel of spruces, skirts a tiny rock beach and enters grassy woods, where you have a 150-degree view of the coast.

After crossing a tiny pebble beach, the path reenters the woods, crosses a slightly larger pebble beach, then reenters the open woods and climbs up a grassy headland, where you'll have the best view of the Walk. This overlook is well situated: It's as far west as, and about 50 feet above, the beaches you just walked along, so you can look north and see, straight ahead, a half-mile of milk-white surf crashing against a half-mile of rockbound coast.

Climbing down from the headland, the path runs through more sunny spruce woodlands. Now nearly level, the trail hugs the shore, often only a few feet above the water, so you'll have many views of the ocean.

About a mile from Western Head Road you'll start to see the Western Ear, the southernmost point on Isle au Haut, ahead on your right.

About 1.3 miles from the road, you'll come to the junction of the southern end of the Western Head Trail and the western end of the Cliff Trail.

Before taking a left on the Cliff Trail, go right and follow a very faint unmarked trail down a tiny ravine. In just a couple of hundred feet you'll reach the ocean. Walk to the left along the ledges and you'll have a close view of the spruce-topped Western Ear. At high tide the Ear is a quarter-mile-wide island. At low tide, it's a knob at the end of a peninsula linked to Isle au Haut by a low, pebbly beach. At that time you can walk across the beach to the Ear and enjoy panoramic views—the west coast of Isle au Haut, where you just walked, the tiny rock islands offshore, the hills of the mainland, and the island's entire southern coast, which stretches from the Western Ear to Eastern Head. If you do cross to the Western Ear, be sure to come back before the tide covers up the beach.

When you're ready, retrace your steps to the Cliff Trail and follow it through a tunnel of young spruces and past rocks and ledges to a tiny, pebbly beach at the head of a little cove.

From there you'll climb back into the woods, go through another spruce tunnel, skirt the bottom of a 20-foot-high ledge, cross a small stream (where you'll have more ocean views) and climb down more ledge to a stream flowing across a rocky beach.

Cross both the stream and the beach and you'll soon come to a ledge with a wide vista—all the way from Eastern Head on your left to Western Head on your right.

Next the trail skirts a tiny cove with foaming surf,

then rolls along the top of a bluff, nearly 100 feet above the ocean. This is the most exciting part of the Cliff Trail. You can see steep cliffs ahead of you, surf crashing on the rocks below them, and Eastern Head, two miles away. The views become wider and more dramatic as you descend into a ravine, then climb back onto the headland. On no other ocean walk in Acadia are you so high above the ocean, yet so close to it, for so long.

About .7 miles from the Western Head Trail the path bends away from the headlands and runs along several 15-foot-high boulders on your right. Also on the right, just after the rocks, is a series of charming pools in a narrow cleft in the ledge.

In just a few feet more, at the base of 20-foot cliffs, the eastern end of the Cliff Trail joins the southern end of Western Head Road.

If you're short of time, you can follow the wide, nearly level road back to Duck Harbor, making this Walk a 4.3-mile loop. Soon after its intersection with the Cliff Trail, the Western Head Road curves along the west shore of Deep Cove, where you'll have another view of Eastern Head. The road reaches Duck Harbor about 1.7 miles from the Cliff Trail.

If you have more time (and stamina) you can turn around and retrace your steps to Duck Harbor. That would make the Walk a 5.2-mile round trip—.9 miles longer than taking Western Head Road all the way back to Duck Harbor but immeasurably more scenic.

28 The Eben's Head & Duck Harbor Trails

This undemanding five-mile round trip highlights the west coast of Isle au Haut. You'll have views of Duck Harbor, Moore's Harbor, the Seal Trap and Isle au Haut Bay, and you'll see a picturesque log cabin beside one of the island's largest cascading creeks.

Like the other Great Walks on Isle au Haut, this one begins in Duck Harbor, at the intersection of Western Head Road and the short trail to the ferry landing.

Follow Western Head Road north toward Duck Harbor, which from here looks more like a mountain lake than an arm of the ocean. The road gradually winds around the head of the harbor, passing a spring on the right and crossing a large, pretty stream cascading into the bay.

On the north side of the harbor, Western Head Road ends at the island loop road. Go left at the intersection and follow the loop road along the north side of the narrow, half-mile-long harbor.

About a quarter-mile from the intersection you'll pass the southern end of the Duck Harbor Trail, on your right. In another 100 feet you'll see the southern end of the Eben's Head Trail in a grassy area on your left.

Follow the nearly level Eben's Head Trail and you'll immediately see Duck Harbor and the ferry landing, on your left, as well as the rock islands in Isle au Haut Bay, which separates Isle au Haut from Vinalhaven Island, to the northwest.

Your wide view of the ocean continues as the trail runs through sunny, grassy spruce woods along the headland. Soon you'll come to an unmarked path that leaves the trail on the left and takes you quickly to a rock promontory at the mouth of Duck Harbor. Here you'll have a sweeping water view up the narrow harbor to your left and across Isle au Haut Bay to your right.

Then the Eben's Head Trail descends to a beach of smooth pebbles, crosses the beach and ascends the ledges on the other side (watch for cairns marking the route).

Now the nearly level trail winds along the tops of low cliffs, where you have continuing ocean views. Three miles offshore is the lighthouse on Saddleback Ledge. Ahead of you is the mouth of Moore's Harbor. In the middle of the large western arm of the harbor is the narrow bay known as the Seal Trap.

About .5 miles from the loop road you'll start to cross another pebble beach. In about 100 feet a cairn marks the spot where the trail turns right. Then the path reenters the woods, curves through a dense stand of small spruce trees and quickly returns to the loop road.

Just a few hundred feet farther, the road comes to the edge of a rocky beach at the edge of a small cove. Across the cove is the Seal Trap; Moore's Harbor is to the right.

Then the road curves to the right and gradually climbs uphill, away from the coast. About .5 miles from the end of the Eben's Head Trail, the road levels off and crosses the Duck Harbor Trail.

Go left on the Duck Harbor Trail, which slowly descends the lower slope of Wentworth Mountain. You'll cross a wet area, then a brook, on half-log boardwalks. Then you'll climb up sunny, picturesque ledges decorated with drifts of small pitch pines and thick clusters of blueberry bushes. In the fall, when the blueberry bushes are deep red, these natural rock gardens are stunning.

About .3 miles from the loop road, the .2-mile-long side trail to Deep Cove leaves the Duck Harbor Trail on the left. If you want to see a small, pleasant spruce-ringed bay, follow the smooth trail as it gently descends to the ocean. As it approaches the cove, it passes through a tunnel of thick, young spruces. Then it crosses, on logs, a stream flowing into the cove and emerges on a rocky beach at the head of the bay.

When you're ready, return to the Duck Harbor Trail, which now runs over rocks and roots as it passes through deep spruce woods.

About .4 miles from the Deep Cove Trail you'll begin to see, through the trees on your left, a tiny inlet on the southern edge of Moore's Harbor.

Then you'll cross the large, cascading Eli's Creek where it rushes around a tiny island. On the south side of the island you'll cross the creek—carefully— on ledges. On the north side you'll cross it on a 20-foot-long wooden bridge.

Follow the north bank of the creek upstream for

about a hundred feet as it cascades down the steep hillside. Almost immediately you'll see a picturesque log cabin beside a large pool in the brook.

After exploring this lovely place, return to the Duck Harbor Trail and follow it over a wet, grassy area on half-log boardwalks. Through the trees on your left you'll see the mile-long Moore's Harbor, the largest harbor on Isle au Haut.

Soon the trail takes you to a pebbly beach where you'll have a 180-degree view, including the long, spruce-covered arms of the harbor, its surf-washed rock islands, and Saddleback Ledge lighthouse in the distance.

After you've enjoyed this view, turn around and follow the trail back to Duck Harbor.

29
Duck Harbor Mountain

This moderate excursion—a 2.4-mile round trip or a 3.2-mile loop, depending on how you return to the trailhead—is a classic Acadian mountain walk. You quickly ascend a low (309-foot) mountain whose ledgy knobs offer continuing panoramic views of the magnificent west and south coasts of Isle au Haut.

Unlike most Great Walks, this one requires bits of steep climbing and occasional hands-and-feet ascents of ledges (and one or two hands-feet-and-fanny descents). But the climbing and scrambling are brief exceptions to an otherwise moderate walk and the extraordinary views justify the periodic inconvenience. This Walk will be most enjoyable if you take it slowly, both to make the climbing easier and to appreciate the views longer.

Like all Great Walks on Isle au Haut, this one begins at the intersection of Western Head Road and the trail to the ferry landing at Duck Harbor.

Follow the grassy Western Head Road as it rises gently through a clearing, past blueberry bushes and spruces. In just a few hundred feet you'll reach the Duck Harbor Mountain Trail, on the left.

The narrow trail immediately starts climbing, over steplike roots and rocks, up the steep slope of the mountain. After just a couple of hundred feet the trail levels off on a wide granite ledge, where you'll enjoy your first views. One hundred feet below you is Isle au Haut Bay. Farther away is Vinalhaven and other islands in Penobscot Bay. In the distance, on the horizon, is the mainland.

Take a right where the trail forks and keep climbing over gray ledges bordered by low spruces, juniper and thick clumps of sheep laurel and blueberries. (Blue blazes and cairns mark the trail.) Your panorama will get longer and wider with almost every step. Soon you'll have a 150-degree view that includes the tree-covered hilly spine of Isle au Haut to the north, the narrow, half-mile-long Duck Harbor below you and some of the many dark green, spruce-covered islands in Isle au Haut Bay.

In just a few minutes you'll reach a granite knob on a shoulder of the mountain, where the view widens to 180 degrees. Now you can also see the ocean on the *east* side of the island, as well as the Camden Hills and other low mountains on the mainland and the buildings around the harbor in Stonington.

The trail leaves the ledge and runs briefly through shady, moss-floored spruce woods before climbing onto a second ledgy knob with even wider views. Now you can see the round-topped, 934-foot monadnock of Blue Hill on the mainland, to the right (east) of Stonington.

Then the trail runs over a series of ledge knobs before reaching the summit, marked by a small, round metal Geodetic Survey marker embedded in the rock. Here you'll see even more of the ocean to the east.

The trail again passes through spruce woods and soon brings you to the first Pudding, one of a half-dozen or so low ledge knobs separated by spruce forest on the southeast ridge of the mountain. Each Pudding has a slightly different ocean view.

The first Pudding offers a 180-degree vista to the west, over Penobscot Bay. From the second you can see the south coast of Isle au Haut, which stretches from Western Head, in the southwestern corner of the island, to Eastern Head, a peninsula in the southeastern end of the island. Just west of Eastern Head is Head Harbor. On the southern horizon is the crisp horizon of an open, islandless sea.

After sliding down the second Pudding on your hands, feet and fanny, you'll pass between large mossy boulders and spruces. Then, on hands and knees, you'll clamber up the third Pudding, where you'll see Western Head; Deep Cove, to the south; and a wide sheet of blue ocean.

At the next Pudding you'll have another view to the south and east and, at the last Pudding, a sweeping, 240-degree view running from the south coast of Isle au Haut all the way to the mainland.

You'll have still more views to the south as the trail descends long, steep ledges. Then you'll pass through nearly level spruce woods and quickly come to the Goat Trail (Walk No. 26) at Squeaker Cove.

If you want to return to the ferry landing, the easiest and probably quickest way is to take the Goat Trail to Western Head Road and, from there, the pleasant (but viewless) Western Head Road back to Duck Harbor. That route would make this Walk a 3.2-mile loop.

A shorter but more difficult route would be simply to go back over Duck Harbor Mountain. That would make the Walk a 2.4-mile round trip. The route would also be much more scenic, though rather more strenuous, than returning by the Goat Trail and Western Head Road.

Honorable Mentions

30 Paradise Hill

This undemanding 1.5-mile round trip takes you to a carriage road 260 feet above French-man Bay, where you'll have a view of Hulls Cove, the Porcupine Islands and Schoodic Peninsula. En route you'll see a 50-foot-long beaver dam and two beaver lodges in a pond off the trail.

This short trip is not a Great Walk because it offers only one view along its entire length. We describe it, however, because the view is excellent, the beaver structures are interesting and the walk is pleasant and relatively short.

The excursion begins at the northwestern end of the parking lot at the park Visitor Center, which is just off Route 3 in Hulls Cove. A sign at the trailhead explains how, between 1915 and 1933, John D. Rockefeller, Jr. "financed and directed" the building of 50 miles of carriage roads in what is now the national park, as well as the roads' "picturesque gate-houses" and "exquisitely designed stone bridges."

The unusually smooth and wide path is almost level as it curves through a pleasant, open mixed forest that includes many small white birches.

About .2 miles from the parking lot, the path turns left and starts climbing Paradise Hill. Here you'll see a pond through the trees on the right of the trail and a rough path leading to it.

Follow the path to the pond and look at the trees and stumps on both sides of the trail. Many bear the marks of beaver teeth.

About 60 feet from the main trail you'll reach the pond and see what the beavers did with at least a few of the trees. On your right is a large beaver dam — 50 feet long and 5 feet high in places. The dam has turned this part of Breakneck Brook into a .2-mile-long pond. The beavers have also built two beaver lodges in the pond; the one closest to you rises at least five feet above the water.

If you'd like to know more about these remarkable builders, inquire at the Visitor Center when you finish your walk.

When you're ready to continue, go back to the main trail and make the gradual but continuous climb up Paradise Hill.

About .5 miles from the parking lot the path ends at a carriage road. Take a left onto the wide, smooth gravelly road, which curves clockwise around the north side of Paradise Hill. (As on all carriage roads, keep an eye out for bicyclists zipping by.) About .7 miles from the parking lot the road reaches the east side of the hill, where suddenly you have a 120-degree view of Frenchman Bay and the eastern shore of Mount Desert Island.

On your left, about .5 miles to the north, is the village of Hulls Cove. Directly below and less than .2 miles away as the gull flies is the park Visitor Center. Almost due east and about four miles away are Burnt Porcupine and Long Porcupine Islands, so close together that from here they look like a single island. To the right of Burnt and Long Porcupine and about three miles from the road is the smaller Sheep Porcupine Island. To the right of Sheep Porcupine, close to shore and only two miles from the road, is Bar Island. Eight miles across the bright blue Frenchman Bay is Schoodic Peninsula.

No other carriage road has an ocean view that rivals this one. After you've enjoyed it, retrace your steps to the parking lot.

31 Long Pond

This easy round trip offers an extended, dramatic lake-and-mountain vista from a nearly level path along Mount Desert Island's largest body of fresh water. Since the path follows Long Pond for almost two miles, you can make this outing as short as one mile (our recommendation) or as long as four miles.

This walk is not a Great Walk because it offers only one view. We describe it, however, because the view is long and worth a look and because the pleasant lakeside trail is one of the park's widest, smoothest and most level paths.

The walk begins at the southern end of Long Pond. To reach the trailhead, take Route 102 to Seal Cove Road; the intersection is about 4.5 miles south ~~~~esville and about .7 miles north of the center ~~~~west Harbor. Turn west on Seal Cove Road ~~~~.6 miles from Route 102, turn right onto

Long Pond Road. About 1.8 miles from Route 102, Long Pond Road ends at a white pumping station beside the pond. As the road descends toward Long Pond you'll see the steep slope of Western Mountain ahead.

If you're driving to the trailhead from the north, you can also take a shorter, more scenic but probably slower route that begins at the intersection of Route 233 and the road to the Eagle Lake swimming area. The intersection is on the west side of Route 233, about two miles north of Southwest Harbor and about four miles south of Somesville. A park sign here says "Echo Lake Entrance." Turn onto the Echo Lake Road and, about .3 miles from Route 233, turn onto the unpaved Lurvey Spring Road, which twists through thick, deep evergreen woods; the speed limit is 15 miles per hour. About 1.6 miles from Route 102 the Lurvey Spring Road ends at Long Pond Road. Turn right onto Long Pond Road, which in another .4 miles brings you to the pumping station at the southern shore of the pond.

Even before you get out of your car, you'll enjoy Long Pond's most dramatic view. Here the four-mile-long lake is less than 1,000 feet wide, squeezed on both sides by the steep, forested slopes of two mountains: 949-foot Mansell—the easternmost summit of Western Mountain, which springs up on the left side of the lake—and 849-foot Beech Mountain (Walk No. 24), which sweeps up on the right.

Leave your car in the parking area beside the lake and walk along the shore toward Mansell Mountain. Near the pumping station (the lake is Southwest Harbor's water supply) you'll see a sign beside the path saying "Great Pond Trail" (Long Pond used to be known as Great Pond).

Keep following the trail as it hugs the shore. You'll immediately cross a brook on a wooden bridge and reach a trail junction. The Mansell Mountain Trail goes to the left; the Great Pond Trail goes straight ahead, close to the shore. Keep going straight. On your right, across the pond, you'll see the fire tower on top of Beech Mountain and bare ledge on the slope of the mountain to the right.

About .2 miles from the pumping station you'll come to another trail junction. The Perpendicular Trail, which also ascends Mansell Mountain, climbs steeply away from the shore path, on the left. Keep following the well-groomed Great Pond Trail, which runs easily over rock slides that have tumbled down Mansell's precipitous face. Above the slides are sheer cliffs. You'll also have nearly continuous views of the pond and the sharp slope of Beech Mountain, just a few hundred feet across the water.

About .5 miles from the pumping station—or whenever you've seen enough of the view—turn around and follow the path back to your car.

32
Norumbega Mountain

This moderate 3.8-mile round trip takes you up a 852-foot peak that offers views of Somes Sound and more than a dozen landmarks around it, including Southwest Harbor, Northeast Harbor, Greening Island, the Cranberry Isles and nine summits: Acadia, Beech, Cedar Swamp, Parkman, Sargent, St. Sauveur and Western mountains and Bald and Gilmore peaks. You'll also see Valley Cove and Long and Lower Hadlock ponds.

This trip isn't a Great Walk because its views are only intermittent and you have to walk too long in the woods to see them. We include it, however, because these views are good and the woods are often pleasant.

The trail—the easiest and most scenic route up Norumbega—begins on an unpaved road on the south shore of Lower Hadlock Pond. The road leaves Route 3 and 198 about .3 miles north of the intersection of Route 3 and Route 3 and 198 in Northeast Harbor and about four miles south of the intersection of Route 3 and 198 and Route 233 at the north end of Somes Sound. The unpaved road is marked only by a sign saying "No Swimming" (Lower Hadlock Pond is Northeast Harbor's water supply). About .1 miles from Route 3 and 198, the road reaches a gate.

Park off the road, to the left of the gate, and start walking along the road. Lower Hadlock Pond is on your right and the east slope of Norumbega Mountain rises on the other side of the pond. Ahead of you is the Northeast Harbor Water Company's red brick pumping station. Very soon you'll see the well-named 974-foot Bald Peak rising above the north shore of the pond.

Then the road forks twice in quick succession. In each case go right. The second right fork will take you close to the pond, where a sign on your left says "Norumbega Mountain."

The road now goes straight to the pumping station. You'll walk along the top of a handsome earth dam faced on its pond side with rectangular granite stones. Then you'll cross the bridge over Hadlock Brook, which drains the pond, and immediately come to the pumping station.

Now the route divides again; the left fork leads to a golf course, the right one follows the shore. Go right.

You'll walk just a few feet more when, about .2 miles from your car, the path splits yet again. The right fork continues around the pond; the left fork, known as the Shady Hill Trail, goes up the mountain.

Follow the Shady Hill Trail as it climbs away from the pond, through a forest of cedar, spruce and pine. Through the trees on your right you'll glimpse the pond and the mountains beyond it.

The pine needle-carpeted path climbs steadily up the top of Norumbega's south ridge, sometimes passing flat, sunny ledges ringed with blueberry bushes. Then it descends gently, levels off and runs through a shady patch of evergreen trees.

Next it climbs steeply to the top of an open ledge, where you have views in three directions. To the east, on your right, is the long north-south ridge of 942-foot Cedar Swamp Mountain. Behind you is the ocean off Northeast Harbor. On the horizon to the west is 1,071-foot Western Mountain, the park's sixth-highest summit. In front of Western Mountain is 839-foot Beech Mountain (Walk No. 24); you can see the fire tower on its summit. In front of Beech Mountain and slightly to the left of the fire tower is the 679-foot summit of St. Sauveur Mountain (Walk No. 23). To the right of St. Sauveur is 681-foot Acadia Mountain (Walk No. 21).

At this point the trail splits again. The left fork goes to the golf course, the right one to the top of the mountain.

Follow the right fork, which goes into the woods again, then climbs steeply to the top of a picturesque rock garden-like ledge, fringed with thick, tight clumps of blueberry bushes and small, shrublike pitch pines. Here you'll have an even wider view than before. You're now high enough to see Valley Cove (Walk No. 22) at the bottom of St. Sauveur Mountain, in Somes Sound. The cove is walled by the nearly vertical Eagle Cliffs, among the steepest cliffs on the island. Behind you are Southwest Harbor, Northeast Harbor, the Cranberry Isles and Greening Island off the mouth of Somes Sound.

Now the trail rolls easily over ledges surrounded by evergreens. Soon you'll have a view of Cedar Swamp Mountain to the east and the slopes of a trio of summits—Bald Peak, 1,036-foot Gilmore Peak and 941-foot Parkman Mountain—to the northeast and 1,373-foot Sargent Mountain (Walk No. 16), the park's second-highest peak, beyond them.

Then you come to an enormous, five-foot-high cairn on an open ledge where you can see mountains in both directions. On the east side of the ridge are the steep, ledgy slopes of Cedar Swamp, Parkman and Sargent mountains and Bald and Gilmore peaks. To the west, on the other side of Somes Sound, are the even steeper bare ledges of Acadia Mountain. Behind Acadia is Long Pond (Walk No. 31). Left of Acadia are the cliffs of St. Sauveur Mountain.

Walk a bit farther and you'll see Somes Sound, including the white houses in the hamlet of Hall Quarry, to the right of Acadia Mountain, and the village of Somesville, at the northern end of the sound.

About .1 miles north of the giant cairn you'll pass the summit of Norumbega. It's marked by a wooden post set in a cairn about 20 feet to the right of the trail.

A few hundred feet beyond the summit, the trail begins its steep descent down the east side of the mountain. Turn around here and enjoy another look at the views as you follow the path back to Lower Hadlock Pond.

To Our Readers:

Please help us stay current. If you discover that anything described in this guide has changed, let us know so we can make corrections in future editions. Please write to: Great Walks, Box 410, Goffstown, NH 03045. Thank you.

Other Great Walks Guides:

▶ *Great Walks of Southern Arizona:* six Great Walks in the fascinating mountains, canyons, and basins of the surprisingly lush Sonoran Desert near Phoenix and Tucson. Great winter walking. 48 pages; 12 full-color photographs; $3.95.

▶ *Great Walks of Big Bend National Park:* six Walks in the Chisos Mountains, the Chihuahuan Desert, and the deep canyons of the Rio Grande, all at the "big bend" of the Rio Grande in the wild open range of southwest Texas. 44 pages; 12 full-color photographs; $3.95.

▶ *Great Walks of the Great Smokies:* 20 Walks to historic sites, impressive waterfalls and cascades, and exciting mountain vistas in Great Smoky Mountains National Park, which straddles the Appalachian Crest in Tennessee and North Carolina. 120 pages; 20 full-color photographs; $5.95.

▶ *Great Walks of Yosemite National Park:* 28 Walks to giant sequoia trees, beautiful lakes, granite domes and other natural rock sculpture, snowcapped 2½-mile-high peaks, and some of the highest waterfalls in the world—all in America's premier national park, in California's Sierra Nevada. 192 pages; 34 full-color photographs; $8.95.

▶ *Great Walks of Sequoia & Kings Canyon National Parks:* 42 Walks featuring large groves of giant sequoias, awesome canyons, panoramic mountain views, fascinating marble caves, and impressive waterfalls in the Sierra Nevada, just a few hours' drive from Yosemite National Park. 208 pages; 33 full-color photographs; $8.95.

▶ *Great Walks of the Olympic Peninsula:* 62 Great Walks and three Honorable Mentions in Washington's Olympic Peninsula, which has more Great Walks than any other region of its size in America. Forty-two Walks are in Olympic National Park, which has more Great Walks than almost any other national park. The trails take you through wildflower-filled mile-high meadows with uninterrupted views of jagged, glacier-covered Olympic mountains; along wild Pacific beaches adorned with seastacks, arches, and other ocean sculpture; through lush temperate rain forests where trees grow as much as 12 feet thick; and to spellbinding waterfalls, cascading streams, and mountain-rimmed lakes. 336 pages; 42 full-color photographs; $13.95.

You can buy Great Walks guides in bookstores or you can order them directly from the publisher by sending a check or money order for the price of each guide you want, plus $1.50 for mailing and handling the order, to: Great Walks, Box 410, Goffstown, NH 03045.

You can also receive more information on the series by sending $1 (refundable with your first order) to Great Walks at the address above.

Own an Original Oktavec Photograph

You can own an original print of any Eileen Oktavec photograph in this guide.

At your request, we will custom make a high-quality, 9¼- by-14-inch color print of your favorite Acadia & Mount Desert Island photograph(s) by the award-winning Eileen Oktavec. The print will be hand labeled, numbered and signed by the photographer. (Because the photograph will be printed on high-gloss paper and much larger than the photograph in the guide, it will be even clearer and more detailed.)

An original Oktavec photographic print is many things: a treasured memento of Acadia, a masterful depiction of its world-famous scenery, a valuable addition to your collection of visual art and, of course, an excellent gift.

To order, simply tell us what print(s) you would like and enclose a check for $76 for each one, plus $4 for shipping and handling any order. Send your order to Great Walks, PO Box 410, Goffstown, NH 03045. Allow 2-3 weeks for delivery.

About the Author
And Photographer

Robert Gillmore and Eileen Oktavec have been taking Great Walks throughout the United States and Europe for years. A landscape designer and author, Gillmore graduated cum laude from Williams and holds a Ph.D. from the University of Virginia. His books include *The Woodland Garden* (Taylor Publishing, 1996).

A photographer, painter, author, and cultural anthropologist, Oktavec graduated from the State University of New York at Stony Brook and has a master's degree from the University of Arizona. She is the author of *Answered Prayers: Miracles and Milagros Along the Border* (University of Arizona Press, 1995), which won a Southwestern Book Award in 1996.

Notice

Every effort has been made to ensure the accuracy of all information in this guide. Nevertheless, due to human and natural factors beyond the control of the author, no Walk described herein can be absolutely risk free. Great Walks Inc. can therefore assume no liability for any accidents or injuries incurred while taking these Walks.